WELCOME

When Allied troops stormed ashore in Normandy on June 6, 1944, their supreme commander, General Dwight D. Eisenhower, inspired them with a message of purpose and dedication.

The supreme commander wrote in his order of the day: "Soldiers, Sailors, and Airmen of the Allied Expeditionary Force!…You are about to embark upon the Great Crusade, toward which we have striven these many months. The eyes of the world are upon you. The hope and prayers of liberty-loving people everywhere march with you. In company with our brave Allies and brothers-in-arms on other Fronts, you will bring about the destruction of the German war machine, the elimination of Nazi tyranny over the oppressed peoples of Europe, and security for ourselves in a free world…."

D-Day was the beginning of the end of World War Two in Europe. As the Red Army inexorably pushed across the frontier of the Fatherland from the east, the Western Allies fulfilled

British men of No. 47 Royal Marine Commando wade ashore at Gold Beach, Normandy, on D-Day. (Public Domain collections of the Imperial War Museums via Wikimedia Commons)

Left: General Douglas MacArthur surveys the landing of American forces on the Philippine island of Leyte in October 1944. (Public Domain National Archives and Records Administration via Wikimedia Commons)

Below: Red Army soldiers rush through the streets of Lvov, Ukraine, during offensive operations in the summer of 1944. (Public Domain Red Army via Wikimedia Commons)

their commitment to Soviet Premier Josef Stalin to open a second front in France. Eleven hard-fought months later, the Nazis were compelled to surrender. However, there were difficult and costly days remaining as the Allies closed in on the black heart of the Third Reich. The Soviets fought and sustained horrendous casualties in their relentless offensives of 1944, while the British and American forces pressed across French Normandy into open country while fighting the Germans in the Low Countries and on the Italian front as well. The stern crucible of the Nazi Ardennes Offensive, the famed Battle of the Bulge, tested the resolve of the Allies at the end of the year but also hastened the demise of the German Wehrmacht as an effective fighting force.

In the Pacific theatre, The forces of imperial Japan were decidedly defeated on land, sea, and air. The Japanese Navy suffered catastrophic defeat in the Battle of the Philippine Sea in June and then the greatest sea fight of the modern era, the Battle of Leyte Gulf, in October. American marines and army troops splashed ashore on tropical islands, wresting control from stubborn defenders who often fought to the death, and General Douglas MacArthur made good on his well-documented promise to the people of the Philippines, stepping forward to declare, "…I have returned."

Welcome to the pages of World War Two: 1944, chronicling the year of Allied offensive might that crushed the Axis enemy and placed the free world on the precipice of final victory over the tyranny of Nazi, Fascist, and totalitarian oppression. Join us in this exploration of a year of sacrifice, heroism, and triumph. This is 1944!

Mike Haskew
Editor

ISBN: 978 1 83632 013 5
Editor: Mike Haskew
Senior editor, specials: Roger Mortimer
Email: roger.mortimer@keypublishing.com
Cover Design: Steve Donovan
Design: SJmagic DESIGN SERVICES, India
Advertising Sales Manager: Sam Clark
Email: sam.clark@keypublishing.com
Tel: 01780 755131
Advertising Production: Becky Antoniades
Email: Rebecca.antoniades@keypublishing.com

SUBSCRIPTION/MAIL ORDER
Key Publishing Ltd, PO Box 300, Stamford, Lincs, PE9 1NA
Tel: 01780 480404
Subscriptions email: subs@keypublishing.com

Mail Order email: orders@keypublishing.com
Website: www.keypublishing.com/shop

PUBLISHING
Group CEO and Publisher: Adrian Cox

Published by
Key Publishing Ltd, PO Box 100, Stamford, Lincs, PE9 1XQ
Tel: 01780 755131 **Website:** www.keypublishing.com

PRINTING
Precision Colour Printing Ltd, Haldane, Halesfield 1, Telford, Shropshire. TF7 4QQ

DISTRIBUTION
Seymour Distribution Ltd, 2 Poultry Avenue, London, EC1A 9PU
Enquiries Line: 02074 294000.

CONTENTS

American troops march down the Champs Élysées during a victory parade following the liberation of Paris. (US Army via Wikimedia Commons)

WELCOME — 3

JANUARY

3 Major Gregory 'Pappy' Boyington shot down — 6
11 Count Ciano executed — 7
22 Operation Shingle: Anzio landings begin — 8
27 Siege of Leningrad ends — 10

FEBRUARY

4 Kwajalein secured — 11
14 General Eisenhower activates SHAEF — 12
15 Destruction of the Abbey of Monte Cassino — 13-14
16 Soviet Union and Finland discuss peace — 15
18 Operation Jericho: bombing Amiens prison — 16
18 US Navy carrier aircraft raid Truk — 17
20 Big Week — 18-19

MARCH

5 Chindit Operation Thursday begins — 20-21
8 Battle of Imphal begins — 22
24 Fosse Ardeatine massacre — 23
30 RAF raid on Nuremberg — 24

APRIL

4 General de Gaulle takes command of Free French forces — 25
21 Badoglio government falls and reforms — 26
22 US forces land at Hollandia and Aitape in New Guinea — 27
27 Exercise Tiger: Slapton Sands tragedy — 28-29
30 B-24 Liberator production peaks at Willow Run — 30
30 State of war: January to April, 1944 — 31-33

MAY

9 Soviet forces liberate Sevastopol — 34
11 Operation Diadem: cracking the Gustav line — 35-36
18 Merrill's Marauders take Myitkyina airfield — 37
25 Allied VI Corps, Fifth Army link up at Anzio — 38-39

JUNE

2 Operation Frantic shuttle-bombing begins — 40
4 U-505 captured on high seas — 41-42
4 Liberation of Rome — 43-44
6 Operation overlord: D-Day — 45-48
10 Oradour-sur-Glane massacre — 49
15 US forces land on Saipan in the Marianas — 50-51
19 Battle of the Philippine sea — 52-53
22 Red Army launches Operation Bagration — 54-55
27 Liberation of Cherbourg — 56

A US Navy fighter pilot flames a Japanese plane during the Battle of the Philippine Sea. The battle's aerial aspect was dubbed the 'Great Marianas Turkey Shoot'. (US Navy via Wikimedia Commons)

British troops move forward from Sword Beach on D-Day, June 6, 1944. (Collections of the Imperial War Museums via Wikimedia Commons)

Above: Inspirational and eccentric leader of the Chindits in the China-Burma-India theatre, Brigadier General Orde Wingate talks with other officers. (Collections of the Imperial War Museums)

Left: General Dwight D. Eisenhower, Supreme Commander of Allied Forces in Europe, and Air Chief Marshal Sir Arthur Tedder, discuss the surrender of Nazi Germany at SHAEF headquarters. (US Army via Wikimedia Commons)

JULY

9	Caen captured	57-58
13	Lvov-Sandomierz offensive begins	59
18	Prime Minister Tojo resigns	60
20	Hitler assassination plot	61-62
21	US forces land on Guam	63
25	Operation Cobra: Normandy breakout	64-65

AUGUST

1	Warsaw uprising	66-67
15	Operation Dragoon: Allies invade southern France	68
15	Allies reach the Gothic Line in Italy	69
18	Red Army reaches East Prussia border	70
21	Battle of Falaise ends	71-72
23	Romanian defences crumble	73
25	Liberation of Paris	74
30	State of war: May to August, 1944	75-77

SEPTEMBER

4	Antwerp liberated	78
5	Dolle Dinsdag	79
8	First V-2 rocket attack	80-81
12	Second Quebec conference begins	82
15	US forces land on Peleliu	83
17	Operation Market Garden begins	84-85
19	Battle of the Hürtgen Forest underway	86-87

OCTOBER

9	Moscow conference	88
14	Rommel commits suicide	89
20	MacArthur returns to the Philippines	92
20	Liberation of Belgrade	93
21	Aachen falls	94
23	Battle of Leyte Gulf begins	95-97

NOVEMBER

1	Operation Infatuate: clearing Walcheren Island	98
4	Sir John Dill dies	99
7	Roosevelt elected to fourth term	100
12	Battleship *Tirpitz* sunk	101
22	British Pacific Fleet established	102
24	First B-29 raid on Japan from the Marianas	103
29	*Archerfish* sinks *Shinano*	104

DECEMBER

14	Palawan massacre	105
15	Glenn Miller goes missing	106
16	Battle of the Bulge begins	107-108
18	Typhoon batters Halsey's third fleet	109
24	SS *Leopoldville* sunk	110
26	Bastogne relieved	111-112

CONCLUSION	113-114

Soviet Marshal Georgy Zhukov (right) and Marshal Semyon Timoshenko led the Soviet Red Army to great victories in 1944. (Mikhail Samoylovich Bernshtein Russian Federation via Wikimedia Commons)

MAJOR GREGORY 'PAPPY' BOYINGTON SHOT DOWN

The fighter sweep over the fortress of Rabaul quickly developed into a wild melee as pilots of VMF-214, the US Marine Corps' fabled 'Black Sheep Squadron', tangled with swarms of Japanese fighters, at least 70 of them, which outnumbered the Americans more than two to one.

Major Gregory 'Pappy' Boyington, commander of VMF-214, was an air combat veteran. At age 31, he was significantly older than his charges, who referred to him affectionately as 'Pappy'. On this day, Boyington pitched into the enemy and quickly shot down two Japanese fighters. Including an estimated six enemy aircraft he had downed in the skies over China as a pilot of the famed American Volunteer Group, better known as the Flying Tigers, his score rose to 28 aerial kills.

However, the tables were turned on Boyington. He was not heard from again that day, or for the duration of the war. He was shot down and presumed killed in action. Months later, when he was presented

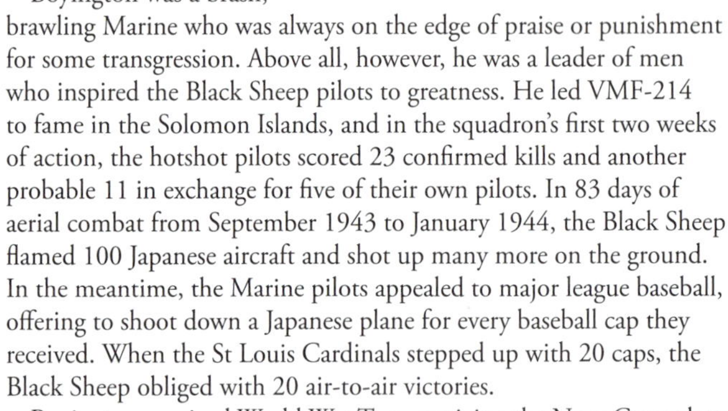

Major Gregory 'Pappy' Boyington strikes a pose prior to a mission in the Pacific. (Public Domain United States Marine Corps via Wikimedia Commons)

the Medal of Honor for heroism, it was assumed that the award was posthumous. But Boyington had survived the shootdown. Fished from the water by the crew of the Japanese submarine I-*181*, he was taken prisoner and held for 20 months before he was liberated – alive – to the astonishment of those who had been in the air with him on that fateful day.

Boyington was a brash, brawling Marine who was always on the edge of praise or punishment for some transgression. Above all, however, he was a leader of men who inspired the Black Sheep pilots to greatness. He led VMF-214 to fame in the Solomon Islands, and in the squadron's first two weeks of action, the hotshot pilots scored 23 confirmed kills and another probable 11 in exchange for five of their own pilots. In 83 days of aerial combat from September 1943 to January 1944, the Black Sheep flamed 100 Japanese aircraft and shot up many more on the ground. In the meantime, the Marine pilots appealed to major league baseball, offering to shoot down a Japanese plane for every baseball cap they received. When the St Louis Cardinals stepped up with 20 caps, the Black Sheep obliged with 20 air-to-air victories.

Boyington survived World War Two, receiving the Navy Cross along with his coveted Medal of Honor. He retired from the Marine Corps in 1947 with the rank of colonel and died in Fresno, California, on January 11, 1988, at the age of 75. His exploits and those of VMF-214 were popularised in the television series *Baa Baa Black Sheep*, which aired in the 1970s. A blend of fact and fiction, the series starred actor Robert Conrad as Pappy Boyington.

Prior to a mission on September 11, 1943, Pappy Boyington briefs pilots of the Black Sheep Squadron. (Public Domain National Museum of the US Navy via Wikimedia Commons)

Pilots of the famed Black Sheep Squadron, VMF-214, stand before a Vought F4U Corsair fighter at their base on the island of Espiritu Santo. (Public Domain National Museum of the US Navy via Wikimedia Commons)

COUNT GALEAZZO CIANO EXECUTED

By early 1944, the fortunes of war had turned decidedly against Italy. Not only had the nation's military suffered humiliating setbacks in Greece and North Africa, but the invasion of Sicily and the mainland of Italy the previous summer had spelled imminent doom for the fascist government of Benito Mussolini, the once swaggering Il Duce who had come to power more than two decades earlier.

Mussolini had appeared before the Fascist Grand Council in July 1943 just days after Allied troops had come ashore in Sicily. The developing crisis led to a vote that ousted Mussolini from power by a wide margin of 18-9. Among those voting to relieve Il Duce that day was Count Galeazzo Ciano, the government's ambassador to the Vatican. Ciano was the son-in-law of Mussolini, married to his daughter Edda, and the country's former foreign minister.

Ciano was a staunch fascist and early advocate of alliance with Nazi Germany. He had flown combat missions with the Italian Air Force during the war with Ethiopia in 1935 and gained political favour, rapidly advancing within the government structure. He was named minister of press and propaganda on his return from the African adventure and then installed as foreign minister on June 9, 1936. Soon enough, however, Ciano began to question the partnership with Hitler, particularly after the invasion of Poland that ignited World War Two in Europe in 1939, which the Nazis undertook without consulting their Axis cohorts.

Following the military embarrassments in Greece and North Africa – the Germans had come to their assistance on both occasions – Ciano advocated for peace. However, his attitude was labelled defeatist, and Mussolini dismissed Ciano as foreign minister in February 1943, appointing him instead to the office of ambassador to the Vatican. A month after the pivotal July 1943 ousting of Il Duce, Ciano, Edda, and their three children fled to Germany to evade arrest by the new government of Italy, which had switched sides and joined the Allies.

Meanwhile, the Nazis rescued Mussolini from imprisonment and installed him as head of a puppet state, the Italian Social Republic, in the north of the country. The Nazis delivered Ciano into the hands of Mussolini, who had his son-in-law charged with treason and arrested. During the subsequent trial in the city of Verona, Ciano was convicted and sentenced to death.

Although Edda pleaded with her father to spare her husband's life, the sentence was carried out on this January morning. Ciano and four others were tied to chairs, and as a further indignity they were to be shot in the back. Just before the fatal shots were fired, Ciano managed to twist his chair slightly, face his executioners, and shout: "Long Live Italy!"

Count Galeazzo Ciano stands at far right during the Munich Conference of 1938. Also pictured are British Prime Minister Neville Chamberlain, French Prime Minister Edouard Daladier, German Chancellor Adolf Hitler, and Italian dictator Benito Mussolini. (Creative Commons Bundesarchiv Bild via Wikimedia Commons)

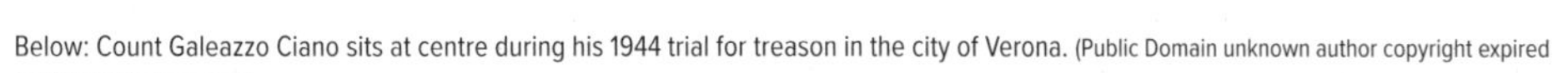

Left: Former Italian Foreign Minister Count Galeazzo Ciano was executed for treason on order of his father-in-law Benito Mussolini. (Public Domain Atelier Binder via Wikimedia Commons)

Below: Count Galeazzo Ciano sits at centre during his 1944 trial for treason in the city of Verona. (Public Domain unknown author copyright expired via Wikimedia Commons)

OPERATION SHINGLE: ANZIO LANDINGS BEGIN

Soldiers of the US 3rd Infantry Division come ashore at Anzio during the opening hours of Operation Shingle. January 22, 1944. (Public Domain US Army via Wikimedia Commons)

The logic was simple, but it was a risky proposition. The long slog up the boot of Italy had cost the Allied Fifth and Eighth Armies dearly in blood and treasure. And the stubborn defence of the Germans remained. Typical of the enemy's tenacity was the stand at the Gustav Line, where firmly entrenched defenders barred the way north to the Italian capital of Rome.

When Prime Minister Winston Churchill had advocated for Allied landings in Italy in mid-1943, he described the offensive as a blow against the "soft underbelly" of Nazi-occupied Europe. As the arduous campaign dragged on, US General Mark Clark, commanding Fifth Army, came to describe the operational area as a "tough old gut."

By January 1944, however, Churchill was again calling for an amphibious operation, this time to outflank the stout defences of the Gustav Line, unhinge the German positions south of Rome, and make

the Eternal City the first Axis capital to fall to Allied forces during World War Two. Therefore, the Allied VI Corps, comprised of the US 3rd and British 1st Infantry Divisions, was designated to assault the beaches at the resort town of Anzio on the coast of the Tyrrhenian Sea, behind the Gustav Line and roughly 35 miles south of Rome. A bold stroke, senior Allied commanders believed, would make tremendous progress toward final victory in the Mediterranean theatre.

General John P. Lucas, commander of VI Corps, was sceptical from the beginning. Code named Operation Shingle, the Anzio landings were to take place along a 15-mile strand of beach. Lucas was cautious and wrote despairingly prior to Shingle: "They will end up putting me ashore with inadequate forces and get me in a serious jam…Then who will get the blame?" Lucas also referenced the disastrous 1915 Dardanelles offensive during World War One when a similar operation, advocated by then-First Lord of the Admiralty Churchill, had utterly failed. He groused that the entire operation held a "strong odour of Gallipoli, and apparently the same amateur…still on the coach's bench."

When the VI Corps vanguard landed at Anzio on January 22, 1944, the Germans were taken completely by surprise. By the end of the day, 36,000 troops were ashore along with 3,200 tanks and other vehicles. Hours later, the number of fighting men rose to 50,000, while only 13 men had been killed with 97 wounded and 44 missing. An aggressive commander might well have recognised the opportunity to sweep rapidly toward Rome as initial German opposition was light. Initial objectives were easily taken, and the beachhead itself was expanded seven miles within two days. Early reports were promising and indicated only sporadic resistance.

However, Lucas was cautious and chose to consolidate his

Left: Landing craft offload supplies for British troops at Anzio during Operation Shingle. (Public Domain collections of the Imperial War Museums via Wikimedia Commons)

Right: Major General John P. Lucas led VI Corps ashore at Anzio on January 22, 1944, and lost his job a month later. (Public Domain US War Department via Wikimedia Commons)

beachhead rather than swiftly advance. In fairness, the VI Corps commander was perplexed by vague orders. General Clark had ordered an advance on the Alban Hills, high ground that dominated Highway 7, the major artery into Rome from the southwest, and about 20 miles inland from Anzio. To the southeast, control of the Velletri Gap would open Highway 6, another route toward the Italian capital. Clark had urged Lucas to operate sufficiently to draw enemy troops away from the Gustav Line to the south, but his orders were not explicit regarding the swift seizure of the Alban Hills.

While Lucas vacillated, the Germans responded quickly to the threat at Anzio. Within 48 hours, Field Marshal Albert Kesselring, the German theatre commander, mobilised elements of several army and Luftwaffe field divisions. The rapid response slammed the door on the Allies, and the German defenders that ringed the Anzio beachhead eventually numbered 135,000. Attack and counterattack yielded only mounting casualties and stalemate.

While Operation Shingle stagnated, Churchill moaned: "I had hoped we were hurling a wild cat onto the shore, but all we got was a stranded whale." As the fighting at Anzio continued, the Allied commitment eventually swelled to 150,000 combat troops and seven full divisions. The British 5th and 56th Infantry Divisions and the American 36th, 45th, and 1st Armored came ashore in the weeks that followed the initial January landings.

General Lucas was relieved of command of VI Corps on February 22, 1944, a month after Operation Shingle was undertaken. General Lucian Truscott was elevated from command of the 3rd Infantry Division to take his place. Perhaps Lucas had engineered his own self-fulfilling prophecy of failure. But most certainly, he should not be singly shouldered with the blame for the lacklustre result of Operation Shingle.

In the event, four months of fighting took place at Anzio, and the successful breakout from the beachhead was accomplished only in concert with Operation Diadem, a major offensive that finally cracked the stubborn defences along the Gustav Line to the south. The cost at Anzio had been frightful for the Allies. Total combat casualties topped 29,000 comprising 4,400 soldiers killed in action, 18,000 wounded, and 6,800 missing in action or captured. Many more men were lost to disease or non-combat related accidents. German losses are estimated at 27,500 with 5,500 dead and 17,500 wounded.

While there is no doubt that Allied soldiers fought bravely at Anzio, their effort was diminished due to circumstances within the higher echelons of command. Therefore, Operation Shingle stands as a sobering example of lost opportunity and what might have been.

A British soldier guards German prisoners captured on January 22, 1944, during the opening hours of Operation Shingle. (Public Domain collections of the Imperial War Museums via Wikimedia Commons)

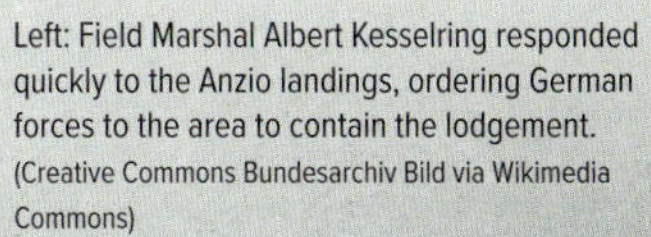

Left: Field Marshal Albert Kesselring responded quickly to the Anzio landings, ordering German forces to the area to contain the lodgement. (Creative Commons Bundesarchiv Bild via Wikimedia Commons)

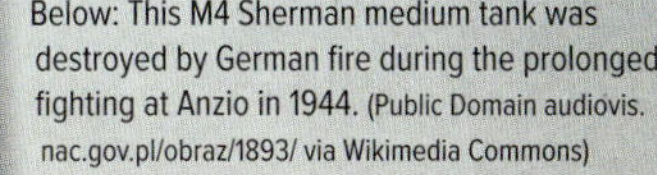

Below: This M4 Sherman medium tank was destroyed by German fire during the prolonged fighting at Anzio in 1944. (Public Domain audiovis. nac.gov.pl/obraz/1893/ via Wikimedia Commons)

SIEGE OF LENINGRAD ENDS

After nearly 900 days of agony, the survivors of the longest siege in modern warfare experienced welcome relief as Red Army troops and tanks finally broke the enemy encirclement of the city of Leningrad. The city had been besieged since September 8, 1941, an objective of German Army Group North and its Finnish allies during the opening days of Operation Barbarossa, Hitler's over-ambitious invasion of the Soviet Union, launched in June of that year. Unable to capture the major population centre in the north of Russia, the invaders chose to lay siege.

In one of the epic events of World War Two, the people of Leningrad withstood months of artillery bombardment, air raids, and German attempts to capture their city, along with the gruelling starvation that took thousands of lives as the population was virtually cut off from resupply for an extended period. In 1942 alone, an estimated 650,000 citizens of Leningrad died of starvation, disease, and exposure to the harsh elements of winter. Only a trickle of supplies reached the city during the ordeal, sometimes coming across the expanse of Lake Ladoga by barge. During winter months when the lake froze solid, trucks managed to cross the surface of ice to open a temporary lifeline, while some supplies were brought into the besieged city by sled. The people remained resolute, refusing to surrender, and one Leningrader wrote: "If you make nails of these people, there will be no harder nails in the world."

At times, the people of Leningrad, now known by its original name of St Petersburg, were reduced to a ration of a mere 125 milligrams of bread per day. Although nearly a million citizens, mainly the elderly and the

Citizens of Leningrad gather in a city street as relief nears in 1944, even though the threat of German artillery fire remains. (Public Domain By Lvova via Wikimedia Commons)

very young, were evacuated as the Nazis approached the city, roughly two million remained, digging anti-tank ditches, and preparing other defences against the invaders. Approximately 200,000 soldiers of the Red Army were prepared to defend Leningrad to the last man as it was encircled by the Germans from the west and south and the Finnish army from the north.

Although meagre supplies reached Leningrad, the suffering of the people was immense. They tried to cultivate small gardens to augment the food supply, and the situation was eased somewhat when the Red Army seized the initiative and offensive operations in 1943 brought some relief. However, months of bitter fighting remained before the final Red Army push during the Leningrad-Novgorod Offensive ruptured the enemy encirclement on January 12 and the Germans were compelled to retreat west from the outskirts of the city. Two weeks later, Soviet troops entered Leningrad, and the arduous siege was lifted. The Soviet government awarded the Order of Lenin to the people of Leningrad in 1945, as estimates of civilian casualties topped one million.

Left: Nurses assist wounded civilians in the streets of Leningrad following a Nazi artillery bombardment. (Creative Commons RIA Novosti via Wikimedia Commons)

Below: During the push toward Leningrad in the summer of 1941, German soldiers pause in front of a burning church. (Public Domain Polish National Archives via Wikimedia Commons)

KWAJALEIN SECURED

After four days of fighting, the island of Kwajalein in the Marshalls archipelago along with neighbouring Roi-Namur to the north fell to American forces. The landings at Kwajalein and Roi-Namur, principally undertaken by the US 4th Marine Division and the US Army's 7th Infantry Division, were components of Operation Flintlock during the progression of the American 'island hopping' strategy across the Central Pacific against the forces of Imperial Japan.

Following the costly victories at Tarawa and Makin in the Gilbert Islands in November 1943, American forces moved on to the Marshalls, where landings took place on February 1, 1944. The 7th Infantry Division, under Major General Charles Corlett, was assigned to take Kwajalein, while the 4th Marine Division, led by Major General Harry Schmidt, assaulted Roi-Namur. Other units involved in the operation included the 22nd Marine Regiment and the Army's 106th and 111th Infantry Regiments.

For two months prior to the landings, American aircraft and naval artillery had steadily bombarded Kwajalein and Roi-Namur, which constituted a portion of the Japanese outer defensive ring in the Pacific. A number of the bitter lessons learned at Tarawa were applied to the subsequent operations in the Marshalls and elsewhere as the war in the Pacific progressed. One American soldier watched the pre-invasion bombardment at Kwajalein and remarked that the "entire island looked as if it had been picked up 20,000 feet and then dropped."

More than 85,000 US troops supported by an armada of over 300 warships and supply vessels reached the Marshalls in late January. Marines stormed ashore on Roi and captured that island within hours. The seizure of Namur followed by noon on February 2. At Kwajalein, the Japanese resistance was more stubborn, and the US Army troops fought for three days before organised resistance ended.

An American soldier stands before an M4 Sherman medium tank at Kwajalein. Sitting atop the Sherman is the hulk of a Japanese Type 94 tank knocked out during the fighting. (Public Domain United States Marine Corps via Wikimedia Commons)

When the battles for Kwajalein and Roi-Namur were over, US casualties had been relatively light with 200 Marines and 177 soldiers killed and 1,500 wounded. The Japanese garrisons were virtually wiped out with 8,500 killed and just over 200 captured. The result of the fighting caused the Japanese to reevaluate their doctrine of heavily contesting the initial landings on invasion beaches, and later US island hopping operations were often subjected to more sophisticated defence in depth.

Soldiers of the US Army's 7th Infantry Division assault a Japanese blockhouse on Kwajalein. (Public Domain US Department of Defense via Wikimedia Commons)

US Marines of the 4th Division advance warily across the scarred landscape at Namur. (Public Domain US Navy via Wikimedia Commons)

GENERAL EISENHOWER ESTABLISHES SHAEF

S HAEF, Supreme Headquarters Allied Expeditionary Force, the Allied military establishment responsible for the invasion of Western Europe and victory over Nazi Germany in World War Two, formally begins operations. Under the command of General Dwight D. Eisenhower, SHAEF guides the pre-invasion planning, the execution of the D-Day landings in French Normandy on June 6, 1944, and the subsequent operations culminating with the surrender of the Nazis in May 1945.

Prior to the formation of SHAEF, planning for the invasion of Western Europe had been underway via COSSAC (Chief of Staff To Supreme Allied Commander), a post occupied by British Lieutenant General Frederick Morgan since March 1943. Morgan served as COSSAC well before a supreme commander was named, and he proceeded afterward with the process that provided the blueprint for Operation Overlord.

After considerable deliberation, President Franklin D. Roosevelt named General Eisenhower as Supreme Commander Allied Expeditionary Force in December 1943. After a brief trip to Washington, D.C., and a visit with his wife Mamie during which he told her: "I'm to command the whole shebang!" Eisenhower returned to Britain on January 15, 1944, to begin the process of converting the COSSAC apparatus to that of SHAEF.

Eisenhower's chief of staff, General Walter Bedell Smith, played a key role in streamlining the cooperative effort that became the SHAEF command

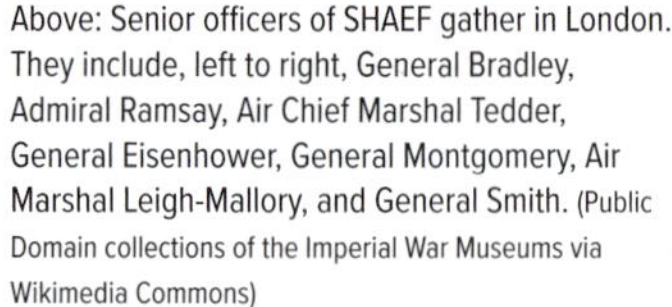

Above: Senior officers of SHAEF gather in London. They include, left to right, General Bradley, Admiral Ramsay, Air Chief Marshal Tedder, General Eisenhower, General Montgomery, Air Marshal Leigh-Mallory, and General Smith. (Public Domain collections of the Imperial War Museums via Wikimedia Commons)

Right: The SHAEF shoulder flash, a familiar symbol of the conflict, is shown on this jacket worn by General Eisenhower during World War Two. (Public Domain US National Archives and Records Administration via Wikimedia Commons)

structure. In the coming weeks, General Eisenhower appointed the senior officers who were to direct the various components of the Allied fighting force that won victory in Western Europe.

Along with Smith, Eisenhower assembled a group of British and American senior commanders including Air Chief Marshal Sir Arthur Tedder of the Royal Air Force as deputy supreme commander, General Morgan as deputy chief of staff, Lieutenant General Humfrey Gale as deputy chief of staff and chief administrative officer, Air Marshal James Robb and Air Vice Marshal Roderick Carr sharing in the posts of deputy chief of staff air forces, General Bernard Montgomery as ground forces commander and commander of 21st Army Group, General Omar Bradley as commander of 12th Army Group, General Jacob Devers as commander of 6th Army Group, Air Marshal Sir Trafford Leigh-Mallory as commander-in-chief air forces, General Hoyt Vandenberg as deputy commander-in-chief air forces, and Admiral Sir Bertram Ramsay as commander-in-chief naval forces.

General Marie-Pierre König and General Ivan Susloparov served as French and Soviet liaison officers, respectively.

After initial operations in London, SHAEF headquarters moved to the European continent, following the Allied ground forces first to Versailles, on the outskirts of Paris, then to the city of Reims, France, and finally to Frankfurt, Germany, following the Nazi surrender. SHAEF operations concluded on July 14, 1945, a day after General Eisenhower delivered to the combined chiefs of staff a report on the organisation's successful completion of its mission.

General Frederick Morgan led the planning for Operation Overlord, the D-Day invasion of Normandy. (Public Domain US Government via Wikimedia Commons)

DESTRUCTION OF THE ABBEY OF MONTE CASSINO

Waves of Allied bombers droned overhead, their target the ancient abbey of Monte Cassino, easily distinguished among the mountaintops that seemed to stretch endlessly across the landscape of southern Italy. The prominent Benedictine monastery that crowned the 1,700ft Monte Cassino massif had been founded by Saint Benedict himself in 529 AD and become the home of the Benedictine order. In one of the most controversial events of World War Two, the 229 Allied aircraft dropped nearly 1,270 tons of high explosives on the landmark, obliterating one of the treasures of Christendom, on February 15, 1944.

The decision to bomb the abbey was not taken lightly by Allied senior commanders. They understood its religious and historical significance. But this was war, and the costly Italian campaign had seen mounting frustration as their forces slogged toward Rome, capital of fascist Italy. Difficult terrain, terrible weather, and determined Nazi resistance had slowed their advance to a crawl. And then in early 1944, the Allies were stymied by the formidable defences of the German Gustav Line, a string of fortifications, machine-gun nests, bunkers, and minefields that ran across southern Italy at its narrowest from northeast to southwest between Ortona on the coast of the Adriatic Sea and Gaeta on the shores of the Tyrrhenian.

Roughly 70 miles south of Rome, the key to the Gustav Line was the town of Cassino on the River Rapido. Cassino was situated astride Highway 6, the main access road to Rome through the valley of the River Liri. For more than a month in January and February 1944, the Allies hammered at the Gustav Line defences around Cassino. Each assault was bloodily repulsed, and finally the attacks which were collectively known as the First Battle of Monte Cassino were halted. Meanwhile, Operation Shingle, an amphibious flanking movement against the Gustav Line at Anzio failed in its objective to compel the Germans to abandon the fortifications to deal with the threat to their rear. In fact, the fighting at the Anzio beachhead devolved into stalemate.

To relieve pressure on the Allied VI Corps at Anzio and hopefully crack the Gustav Line, another heavy attack, known as the Second

An American Boeing B-17 Flying Fortress bomber flies above the smouldering rubble of the abbey of Monte Cassino, February 15, 1944. (Public Domain US Air Force via Wikimedia Commons)

Battle of Monte Cassino, got underway in mid-February. However, prior to this second effort numerous Allied officers had become concerned that the abbey was being used by the Germans as an artillery observation post, and several called for its destruction. Chief among them was New Zealander, General Bernard Freyberg, commander of the 2nd New Zealand,

Left: The ruins of the abbey of Monte Cassino stand starkly against the sky after the bombing of February 15, 1944. (Public Domain collections of the Imperial War Museums via Wikimedia Commons)

Right: New Zealand General Bernard Freyberg was a vocal proponent of the bombing of the abbey of Monte Cassino. (Creative Commons Archives of New Zealand via Wikimedia Commons)

On the day before the bombing of the abbey of Monte Cassino, General Sir Harold Alexander talks with British and American officers at Anzio, Italy. (Public Domain collections of the Imperial War Museums)

Tough German airborne troops like these occupied the ruins of the abbey of Monte Cassino. (Public Domain National Digital Archives of Poland via Wikimedia Commons)

4th Indian, and 78th British Divisions that were slated to conduct the renewed attacks.

In addition to its religious significance, the abbey was renowned as a centre of learning and culture. The Italian government had declared it a national monument in 1886, but there was enough concern regarding its usefulness to the enemy to warrant the bombing, and the final approval came from General Sir Harold Alexander, commander of Allied 15th Army Group. The Germans had actually agreed to respect the sanctity of the abbey and had previously transported many of its precious works of art and manuscripts to the safety of the Vatican. They were not, in fact, occupying the venerable structure at the time of the devastating air raid.

However, once the destruction of the abbey was complete, the Germans did occupy its ruins. And when the Allied ground troops renewed their attacks at Cassino with a preliminary assault on the night of February 16, they ran into the tough Fallschirmjäger of the 1st Parachute Division. In the bitter fighting, the Royal Sussex Regiment, one of the British units assigned to the 4th Indian Division, lost 12 of its 15 officers and 162 of its 313 troops killed or wounded in just 48 hours.

Freyberg's main effort began on February 17 with the 4th Battalion, 6th Rajputana Rifle Regiment and 1st Battalion, 9th Gurkha Rifles hitting secondary objectives while the 1st Battalion, 2nd Gurkha Rifles attacked directly toward the ruins of the abbey. These assaults were brutally repulsed with heavy losses and called off the next day. Elsewhere, elements of the New Zealand 28th Māori Battalion crossed the Rapido and captured the railroad station in the town of Cassino. The 28th held on for several hours before a German counterattack supported by tanks forced them to give up the railway station and retire.

The Second Battle of Monte Cassino ended in frustration for the Allies, while the devastated abbey had become another German stronghold. Two more attempts were made to break the Gustav Line at Cassino before success was achieved in May.

In the end, the destruction of the abbey of Monte Cassino was tragic; however, it had been spawned by the exigencies of war. Actually, a frank examination of the circumstances made the fact that the Germans had not occupied the structure a moot point.

Major General Howard Kippenberger, commander of the New Zealand 2nd Division, offered this contemporary analysis: "If not occupied today, it might be tomorrow, and it did not appear it would be difficult for the enemy to bring reserves into it during an attack or for troops to take shelter there if driven from positions outside. It was impossible to ask troops to storm a hill surmounted by an intact building such as this, capable of sheltering several hundred infantry in perfect security from shellfire and ready at the critical moment to emerge and counterattack…On the whole I thought it would be more useful to the Germans if we left it unbombed."

Rebuilt after World War Two, the abbey of Monte Cassino occupies its prominent location today. (Creative Commons Ludmila Pilecka via Wikimedia Commons)

SOVIET UNION AND FINLAND DISCUSS PEACE

Finnish soldiers advance against the Soviets during fighting in the autumn of 1941. (Public Domain Tauno Norjavirta/SA-kuva via Wikimedia Commons)

On February 16, 1944 Finnish diplomat Juho Paasikivi began a round of discussions with representatives of the Soviet Union regarding peace between the two countries. Travelling to the Swedish capital of Stockholm, Paasikivi was aware that the military situation had deteriorated significantly since Finland cast its lot with Nazi Germany in an obvious effort at self-preservation.

Finland had been a target of an expansionist Soviet Union since the 1920s, and from November 1939 to March 1940, the two countries had fought the brief but brutal Winter War. Although the small but efficient Finnish Army had taken an immense toll on the Soviet invaders, peace terms had been harsh with the Finns making significant territorial concessions, having failed to secure support from Great Britain and France.

Although a formal military alliance was not initially concluded, Finland turned to Germany for enhanced national security. When the Nazis launched Operation Barbarossa, the invasion of the Soviet Union, on June 22, 1941, the Finns allowed German troops to transit their territory and then joined the invaders, hoping to recover their lost lands. The Finnish Army took up positions during the lengthy siege of the Soviet city of Leningrad. Their active military participation being dubbed 'The War of Continuation'.

Wearing uniforms and carrying weapons supplied by Nazi Germany, Finnish soldiers pass a destroyed Soviet T-34 tank in 1944. (Public Domain Finnish Wartime Photograph Archive via Wikimedia Commons)

However, concerns regarding the course of the conflict surfaced within the Finnish government in Helsinki, particularly after the German defeat at the Battle of Stalingrad, the Allied invasions of Sicily and the Italian mainland, and the Soviet victory at Kursk on the Eastern Front, each of these occurring by mid-1943. Finnish Prime Minister Edwin Linkomies formed a new government in March of that year with the goal of extricating the country from its diplomatic and military predicament.

Late in 1943 and into 1944, preliminary discussions regarding a Finnish-Soviet peace accord were conducted. For the Finns, the overture gained renewed urgency when the Red Army lifted the siege of Leningrad in January 1944, and German Army Group North was pushed back to the frontier of the Baltic state of Estonia. Then, while the discussions in Stockholm were underway, major Soviet bombing raids were conducted against Helsinki. Although the damage was relatively light, the implications were clear.

Predictably, initial Soviet demands for a separate peace with Finland were unacceptable. The talks were concluded, but a month later Paasikivi and a Finnish delegation flew to Moscow to meet with Soviet Foreign Minister Vyacheslav Molotov. Again, the peace terms were deemed as intolerable. After formally rejecting the Soviet demands, the Finns left the negotiating table in April 1944.

By autumn, though, the Finnish government was compelled to accept an armistice. Signed on September 19, 1944 the agreement specified that Finland would abide by the terms of the 1940 Treaty of Moscow that ended the Winter War while German troops were to be ejected from Finnish territory. A formal peace treaty between the Soviet Union and Finland was finally signed in Paris on February 10, 1947.

Finnish flags fly at half-mast in Helsinki following the end of the Winter War in 1940. (Public Domain Finnish Wartime Photograph Archive via Wikimedia Commons)

OPERATION JERICHO: BOMBING AMIENS PRISON

The Mosquitos, 18 fighter bombers manned by crews of British, New Zealand, and Australian air squadrons, swept low and fast toward the prison at Amiens, France, where intelligence reports indicated that the Nazi Gestapo was holding more than 1,000 captives, many of them members of the French Resistance.

The weather was terrible, and the twin-engine De Havilland aircraft, built for speed and lethality, were buffeted by high winds, snow, sleet, and rain as they clawed into the air from their British base. But this mission was born of desperation, as the prisoners were apparently scheduled for execution – perhaps even within hours. Operation Jericho, a scheme to bomb the prison at Amiens, 72 miles north of Paris, in broad daylight and at least give the condemned captives a chance to escape, had been conceived by 28-year-old Royal Air Force Group Captain Percy Charles Pickard, a recipient of the Distinguished Service Order with two bars and the Distinguished Flying Cross.

As Pickard saw it, Operation Jericho was the only way to help the prisoners, and the Mosquito was just the plane for the job. Nicknamed the 'Wooden Wonder', the multi-role Mosquito was constructed of birch, spruce, balsa, and plywood. It cruised at 325mph, and at full throttle the twin-engine aircraft could reach 425mph. The plane was also well armed with four .303-calibre machine guns and a pair of 20mm cannon for air-to-air combat, while variants were also capable of delivering a bombload of up to 4,000lb.

On the morning of February 18, 1944, Pickard and company brushed off the bad weather, and he led the flight at low altitude across the English Channel. The leader had told the stout-hearted aircrews: "It's a death-or-glory show, boys. If it succeeds, it will be one of the most worthwhile 'ops' of the war. If you never do anything else, you can still count this as the finest job you have ever done."

The precision strike was right on time and target, blasting the walls of Amiens Prison. Eighty-seven prisoners died in the attack, but others were observed sprinting across the courtyard toward a large breach in the outer wall. More than 250 managed to escape amid the confusion. However, Pickard and his co-pilot were killed when their Mosquito was shot down by a German fighter. One other Mosquito was lost along with two escorting Hawker Typhoon fighter bombers.

French Resistance leader Raymond Vivant and a dozen of his close comrades were among those who made good their escape. Despite the loss of Pickard, among the best-known pilots of the RAF in World War Two, the Air Ministry in London hailed Operation Jericho as "one of the most memorable achievements of the Royal Air Force."

Above: Smoke billows from the prison at Amiens during Operation Jericho. (Public Domain United Kingdom Government via Wikimedia Commons)

Left: De Havilland Mosquitos roar over Amiens prison as their bombs fall during Operation Jericho. (Public Domain United Kingdom Government Imperial War Museum via Wikimedia Commons)

Right: RAF Group Captain Percy Charles Pickard led Operation Jericho and lost his life in the raid. (Public Domain United Kingdom Government via Wikimedia Commons)

US NAVY CARRIER AIRCRAFT RAID TRUK

After two days of incessant attacks from carrier-based aircraft of the US Navy's Task Force 58, the Japanese island fortress and naval anchorage at Truk, in the Carolines archipelago, is left a smoking ruin while many vessels are sunk or disabled in its lagoon.

Japan had taken control of Truk from Germany during World War One and held the island during the interwar years via mandate from the League of Nations. During that time, Truk was heavily fortified and earned the nickname 'Gibraltar of the Pacific'. Since the outbreak of World War Two, Truk had provided the Imperial Japanese Navy with a significant base of operations in the Central Pacific.

By early 1944, Admiral Chester Nimitz, commander-in-chief of the US Pacific Fleet, and his senior officers had concluded that American aircraft carrier strength was sufficient to strike a blow against Truk that would greatly diminish its effectiveness. From that conclusion, Operation Hailstone was devised. Under the command of Admiral Raymond A. Spruance, three of Task Force 58's carrier task groups led by Admiral Marc A. Mitscher were ordered to carry out the heavy air attacks, which coincided with the US amphibious landings on the island of Eniwetok in the Marshalls, roughly 800 miles to the south, and were expected to also suppress any attacks from Truk-based Japanese planes that might oppose those landings.

Japanese ships are caught in the onslaught of American warplanes at Truk Lagoon during Operation Hailstone. (Public Domain US Navy via Wikimedia Commons)

The three US Navy task groups included four Essex-class fleet carriers, *Essex*, *Yorktown*, Bunker *Hill*, and *Intrepid*, along with the Yorktown-class carrier *Enterprise*, the Independence-class light carriers *Cowpens*, *Monterey*, *Cabot*, and *Belleau Wood*, and escorts of six fast battleships, 10 heavy and light cruisers, and 28 destroyers. Altogether, the carriers transported 500 planes.

Operation Hailstone commenced before dawn on February 17, 1944, as 72 fighters were launched in a sweep over the island. The Japanese were taken by surprise but managed to get 90 aircraft aloft. Thirty of these were shot down, and another 40 enemy planes were destroyed on the ground. When the American bombers arrived in the first of 30 separate airstrikes on the day, few if any Japanese fighters rose to defend against them. The attackers ranged virtually at will, sinking, or disabling numerous vessels in the lagoon and hitting shore installations. Specially-equipped bombers conducted raids through the night, and waves of US aircraft continued the onslaught throughout the following day.

When Operation Hailstone concluded, US pilots had flown 1,250 combat sorties, dropped nearly 500 tons of bombs and torpedoes, and sunk two Japanese light cruisers, four destroyers, and an array of other warships and supply vessels. An estimated 275 Japanese aircraft were destroyed. In exchange, the US Navy lost 25 planes, 40 men killed in action, one aircraft carrier and one battleship slightly damaged. Carrier-based air power had effectively neutralised Truk.

US Navy aircraft are prepared for launch aboard the carrier USS *Intrepid* during Operation Hailstone. At right are Vought F4U Corsairs fighters, while Grumman F6F Hellcats are at left. (Public Domain US Navy via Wikimedia Commons)

A plume of water stretches skyward as a US Navy torpedo strikes a Japanese freighter in Truk Lagoon. (Public Domain US Navy via Wikimedia Commons)

BIG WEEK

Six days of sustained bombing by the US Eighth and Fifteenth Air Forces based in Italy marked the resumption of the American daylight strategic bombing campaign against the Third Reich, while the RAF continued its nocturnal raids. Officially known as Operation Argument, 'Big Week' followed a pause in the air effort after the Eighth Air Force had experienced serious losses during raids against heavily defended targets inside Nazi Germany in the autumn of 1943.

Big Week signalled a change in tactics as the bombers were not only expected to cripple German fighter aircraft production with the destruction of assembly plants and factories that produced components, but also to literally serve as bait, luring Luftwaffe pilots into the air to attack the big bomber formations. In the process, Allied air commanders believed that British and American fighter pilots would erode the combat efficiency of the enemy fighter defences through attrition. German synthetic oil production was another target, while air superiority was also a prerequisite for the security of the upcoming D-Day invasion of northwest Europe slated for the spring of 1944.

In December 1943, General Henry 'Hap' Arnold, commander of US Army Air Forces, declared to his subordinates, outgoing Eighth Air Force commander General Ira C. Eaker and incoming commander General Jimmy Doolittle: "…My personal message to you – this is a MUST – is to destroy the enemy air force wherever you find them, in the air, on the ground, and in the factories." When Doolittle replaced Eaker in January 1944, he stressed the Allied fighters would be allowed to range ahead of bomber formations to hunt and destroy German fighters. Although the bomber crews were dismayed to see their escorts flying distant from their box formations, the tactic proved effective.

B-17 Flying Fortress bombers drop their payloads on a target in Nazi Germany in 1944. (Public Domain US Air Force via Wikimedia Commons)

Operation Argument was delayed initially by bad weather, but the storm of Allied bombing broke loose from February 20-25, 1944, and during that period the Eighth and Fifteenth Air Forces flew 3,800 combat missions and dropped 10,000 tons of bombs, significantly more than the Eighth had delivered on enemy targets during its entire first year of operations. Combined Allied bomber and fighter sorties during Big Week totalled more than 6,000.

The weather was less than ideal when 1,000 bombers took off from bases in the Midlands and East Anglia on the first day of Big Week to hit a dozen targets in Germany related to the aircraft production industry. Swarms of Allied fighters, 660 of them, flew in formations that were 25 miles wide, and some ventured up to 50 miles ahead of the bombers in their search for Luftwaffe fighters to engage. A day later, General Doolittle sent 767 heavy bombers against aircraft factories at Brunswick, Germany, while numerous Luftwaffe airfields were also targeted. Only three bombers were lost during the day's action.

On February 22, General Doolittle dispatched 250 Eighth Air Force Boeing B-17 Flying Fortress and Consolidated B-24 Liberator heavy bombers to attack the Junkers aircraft manufacturing plant in the city of Halberstadt, while the Messerschmitt assembly factory in the city of Regensburg, where many Allied bombers had been shot down in August 1943, was also struck. An hour after the B-17s departed, 84 B-24s of the Fifteenth Air Force, flying from bases around Foggia, Italy, followed up at Regensburg. Post-raid assessment indicated that the facilities there had been heavily damaged, but the price was high as 35 B-17s and 13 B-24s were shot down. The Eighth Air Force lost a total of 41 planes as six more that managed to return to bases in England were deemed unflyable.

Left: Bursts of German antiaircraft fire blacken the skies amid formations of American bombers. (Public Domain US Air Force via Wikimedia Commons)

Below: A Boeing B-17 Flying Fortress bomber of the US Eighth Air Force sits at an airfield in Britain. (Public Domain collections of the Imperial War Museums via Wikimedia Commons)

The raids continued despite weather that was less than ideal, and during night attacks on February 24, RAF Avro Lancaster and Handley Page Halifax heavy bombers struck the ball bearing factories at Schweinfurt, Germany, another heavily defended target where many an American bomber had come to grief during terrible daylight raids just months earlier. Through the course of Big Week, the RAF flew more than 2,300 nocturnal missions and dropped 9,200 tons of bombs, while 157 planes were lost to Luftwaffe night fighters and anti-aircraft fire.

On the last day of Big Week, Eighth Air Force B-17s and B-24s struck Schweinfurt and Regensburg yet again along with ball bearing production facilities at Stuttgart. Thirty-one big bombers were lost in the process.

When Big Week was over, more than 2,500 Allied airmen had been killed, wounded, or captured, while 357 bombers and 28 fighters had been lost to enemy action in six days. However, the Luftwaffe had

Above: With an engine smoking, a B-24 Liberator bombers emerges from a curtain of flak over a target. (Public Domain US Air Force via Wikimedia Commons)

Right: General Jimmy Doolittle, commander of Eighth Air Force, instituted aggressive fighter tactics during Big Week. (Public Domain US Air Force via Wikimedia Commons)

suffered mightily, losing 262 fighters destroyed and another 150 damaged. At least 250 German fighter pilots were killed, wounded, or captured, and among these were an estimated 100 veteran fliers whose experience could not be replaced.

Allied assessment of the Big Week raids indicated that enemy fighter production was set back at least two months. But German industry proved resilient as deliveries of new aircraft rebounded and actually exceeded the number completed prior to Operation Argument. Output rose to approximately 1,500 new fighters in the spring of 1944 as some factories were relocated to the protection of caves or underground spaces, safe from Allied bombing.

Nevertheless, Big Week marked the beginning of the end for the Luftwaffe. While scores of its experienced fighter pilots had been killed in action, those who remained were stretched to breaking point in defence of the Reich against the relentless Allied air raids. The increasing number of available Luftwaffe fighters was countered with the lack of experienced pilots to fly them, and many went down in flames under the guns of seasoned RAF and US Army Air Forces pilots.

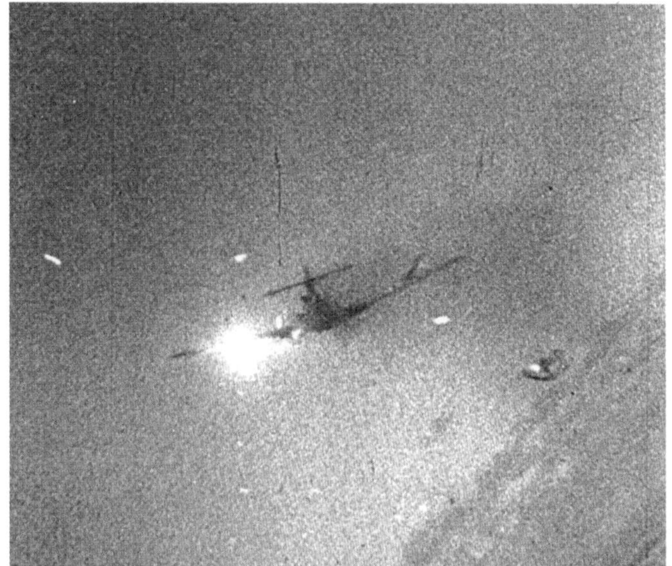

A German Messerschmitt Me-109 fighter bursts into flames under the guns of an Allied fighter in 1944. (Public Domain US Air Force via Wikimedia Commons)

CHINDIT OPERATION THURSDAY BEGINS

The ambitious undertaking dubbed Operation Thursday began inauspiciously in the jungles of Burma as the glider insertion of Chindit troops went awry. Several Douglas Dakota transports, their engines overtaxed while towing two gliders each, crashed. The landing zone designated Piccadilly, still strewn with logs and stumps, was not ready to receive incoming aircraft, and those originally assigned to Piccadilly were diverted to another, Broadway, where only 35 of 61 gliders managed to land without damage.

Regardless, Operation Thursday proceeded. After all, the Chindits had trained to fight in the harshest of conditions.

Their leader, the charismatic Brigadier Orde Wingate, was a superb tactician and veteran of irregular operations, having commanded Gideon Force in East Africa during the early months of World War Two. Wingate, although eccentric, was also a brilliant and innovative officer. Following the success of Gideon Force, he had suggested the formation of a similar unit to be deployed in the China-Burma-India (CBI) theatre. These troops would fight behind Japanese lines in Burma, disrupting communications, destroying supplies, and inflicting casualties on the enemy.

By late 1942, Wingate had recruited and trained a force of 3,000 men, officially designated as the 77th Indian Infantry Brigade. Their commander, however, nicknamed them 'Chindits', a corruption of the Burmese 'chinthe', the mythical lions that were prominent in the art and architecture of the Burmese people.

In mid-February 1943, Wingate's Chindits undertook their first offensive mission, crossing the River Chindwin near the town of Imphal and moving from India into Burma. For the next two months, they operated behind Japanese lines intent on cutting the rail and supply lines that sustained the enemy. In addition to sharp clashes with Japanese troops that had been reoriented to deal with the unexpected threat, the Chindits were obliged to make long marches in the stifling jungle heat, tortured by mosquitoes that carried debilitating malaria. As resupply became increasingly difficult and casualties mounted, Wingate divided the Chindits into small groups to more easily exfiltrate to safety in India, avoiding concentrations of enemy soldiers.

The Chindits conducted a fighting retreat, but their ranks were dangerously thinned. More than

Eccentric and visionary Brigadier Orde Wingate led the Chindit clandestine operations. (Public Domain US Military Photo via Wikimedia Commons)

Chindits cross a river in Burma during their first operation behind Japanese lines in 1943. (Public Domain collections of the Imperial War Museums via Wikimedia Commons)

Chindits board an RAF Dakota transport plane during Operation Thursday. (Public Domain United Kingdom Government via Wikimedia Commons)

Orde Wingate and Chindit officers are shown at landing zone Broadway during Operation Thursday. (Public Domain collections of the Imperial War Museums via Wikimedia Commons)

Marauders and the Chinese forces that would oust the Japanese from northern Burma, seize the key airfield at Myitkyina, and open an overland supply route between India and China. In the event, Operation Thursday would also complicate Japanese plans for an invasion of India.

The Chindits hacked their landing zones and supply bases out of the jungle. Along with Piccadilly and Broadway, there were others including Aberdeen and White City. The labour-intensive effort and thick jungle made maintaining the original timetable problematic, and the opening phase of Operation Thursday was disappointing. Brigadier Bernard Ferguson's 16 Brigade required 23 days to reach the River Chindwin, the halfway point in its planned trek.

Meanwhile, the enemy was alerted. Lieutenant General Masakuzu Kawabe led 10 battalions of Japanese troops against the Chindit supply bases. While two battalions hit Broadway, more than 6,000 enemy soldiers assaulted White City. The pugnacious Brigadier Mike Calvert led 77 Brigade in a ferocious defence often involving hand-to-hand fighting. Calvert audaciously captured the town of Mogaung in June, but combat losses reduced 77 Brigade to fewer than 2,000 men. Chindit 111 Brigade maintained a grim hold on a quickly constructed strongpoint named Blackpool.

These stout efforts gained some time, but tragedy had struck on March 24. Wingate had flown into Aberdeen to assess the situation at the base, and during the return flight he was killed when his aircraft crashed into a mountainside southwest of Imphal.

By mid-August, it was clear that the Chindits should be withdrawn. They had sustained nearly 5,000 casualties, roughly half the number of troops engaged. Historians continue to debate the cost versus the return regarding Chindit operations. However, there is no doubt that their contribution to final victory in the CBI was significant.

800 casualties had been sustained; however, they had earned the grudging respect of their enemies.

In the wake of the first Chindit operation, some senior British officers raised serious doubts about the commitment of manpower to such forays in the future. Refusing to be dissuaded, Wingate was buoyed by the positive aspects of the first Chindit mission, including the fact that Prime Minister Winston Churchill praised the endeavour as a morale booster following a string of Japanese victories in the CBI. Wingate was promoted major general, and the Chindit force was augmented to 20,000 troops.

Churchill, an advocate of special operations from the beginning, remained favourable to the concept of long-range deep penetration missions, and during the Quebec Conference of August 1943, Wingate proposed another, this time in cooperation with the elite American force known as Merrill's Marauders and Chinese troops under the command US General Joseph Stilwell.

Field Marshal Claude Auchinleck, British Commander-in-Chief India, objected, stating: "In my opinion the proposal is unsound and uneconomical as it would break up divisions which will certainly be required for prosecution of the main campaign of 1944/45." But Wingate prevailed, and Churchill later wrote that the "high command in India had been dragging its feet far too long…Wingate won the contest hands down…."

The second Chindit offensive, Operation Thursday involved the prepositioning of supplies at six sites behind Japanese lines. Once the Chindits were on the ground in sufficient numbers, they would sever enemy supply lines, attack communications centres, and engage Japanese troops when the numbers were favourable. Resupply would be conducted by air. While the Chindits wreaked havoc in the Japanese rear, Stilwell would coordinate complementary operations of Merrill's

Brigadier Mike Calvert of Chindit 77 Brigade gives orders during fighting at Mogaung. (Public Domain collections of the Imperial War Museums via Wikimedia Commons)

Chindits make a bivouac during a long-range deep penetration mission behind Japanese lines. (Public Domain collections of the Imperial War Museums via Wikimedia Commons)

BATTLE OF IMPHAL BEGINS

During the opening hours of Operation U-Go, the intended invasion of India, Japanese forces attacked positions of the British 14th Army along a 300-mile front on the plain of Imphal. Fighting raged in early March, 1944 as the attackers laid siege to the town of Imphal, determined to break through and proceed with their offensive to conquer the jewel in the crown of the British Empire.

Along with the battle of Kohima, fought concurrently, the fight at Imphal constituted the turning point of the Allied campaign in Burma during World War Two. General William Slim, commanding the 14th Army, had seen Allied offensive operations in the China-Burma-India (CBI) theatre progress in recent months as forces under the command of US General Joseph Stilwell took the city of Myitkyina and reached the Burma Road while units of the 15th Corps approached the Burmese province of Arakan, and the Chindits under Brigadier Orde Wingate conducted long-range, deep penetration raids behind Japanese lines.

Slim had taken command of the 14th Army in mid-1943 and set about rebuilding its 500,000 troops as an effective fighting force. Early defeats had left morale at its nadir, while the army was low on the list of priorities for new weapons and equipment. Nevertheless, Slim had won the men over with his optimism and command presence.

General Sir William Slim commanded the 14th Army during the pivotal battles of Imphal and Kohima. (Public Domain collections of the Imperial War Museums via Wikimedia Commons)

He visited individual units and spoke to Commonwealth soldiers in their native languages, including Urdu and Gurkhali. When the time was right, Slim employed elements of the 14th Army in limited actions that brought small victories.

Just as Slim contemplated the expanded offensive, the Japanese were wary and struck first, launching Operation U-Go. While the defenders at the town of Imphal were besieged, Slim called for reinforcements and his troops were largely resupplied by air. As British forces fought to reach Imphal, the battle for the town of Kohima raged for a month from mid-April into May, when the Japanese finally pulled back after suffering 6,000 casualties. Weeks of costly fighting lay ahead until the 2nd and 5th Indian Divisions cleared the vital Imphal-Kohima Road and linked up with the defenders at Imphal, lifting the siege on June 22, 1944. The Japanese retreated across the River Chindwin after losing 53,000 soldiers killed, wounded, or captured, and the victories at Imphal and Kohima rank among the most significant Allied triumphs of the conflict.

Slim and his 14th Army pursued the enemy across the Chindwin later in 1944 and unleashed the decisive offensive of the war in the CBI early the following year.

Above: Commonwealth soldiers meet on the Imphal-Kohima road, lifting the siege of Imphal. (Public Domain collections of the Imperial War Museums via Wikimedia Commons)

Below: Gurkha troops and tanks fight the Japanese along the Imphal-Kohima road. (Public Domain United Kingdom Government via Wikimedia Commons)

The entrance to the Ardeatine Caves includes a memorial to those slain in the massacre of March, 1944. (Creative Commons antmoose via Wikimedia Commons)

FOSSE ARDEATINE MASSACRE

On March 24, 1944, Nazi troops rounded up 335 Italians, some of them already held as prisoners and others snatched off the streets of Rome, marched them to the Ardeatine Caves on the outskirts of the capital city, and summarily executed them in reprisal for a partisan attack against an SS security detail the previous day.

On March 23, Rosario Bentivegna, a communist partisan dressed as a sanitation worker, had detonated a bomb containing 40 pounds of TNT in the path of 150 SS-led fascist police officers returning from a training exercise along the Via Rosselli, a single-lane cobblestone street near Rome's Spanish Steps and the Trevi Fountain. Thirty-three Fascist troops were killed outright and more than 100 wounded. A total of 42 fatalities were recorded after others died in hospital. Among those killed were two innocent civilians, one of them just 13 years old.

Partisan groups had regularly conducted operations against the German occupiers in Italy and their Italian Fascist partners during World War Two. And Bentivegna made good his escape, but Nazi retribution was swift. SS Obersturmbannführer Herbert Kappler, commander of the SD, the security arm of the SS, and the fascist police in Rome, immediately received permission from Hitler to punish the Italian people and attempt to deter future such attacks.

German and Italian soldiers round up victims for execution in reprisal to the bombing of March 23, 1944. The victims were murdered the following day. (Creative Commons Bundesarchiv Bild via Wikimedia Commons)

Kappler issued orders to gather 330 prisoners, 10 for each victim of the bombing as determined at the time, and the soldiers apprehended 335, just over their quota. Among these were 57 Jews. The oldest detainee is 70, and the youngest only 15. No effort was made to link any of these individuals to the actual bombing.

The captives were herded to the Ardeatine Caves, an ancient site where Christian martyrs were once buried, taken inside in groups of five, and murdered with a single shot to the back of the head. Each successive group, hands bound, was made to kneel atop the corpses of those already slain. When the barbaric retribution is completed, the Nazis detonated explosives to seal the mouths of the caves and cover up the atrocity.

However, the war crime was uncovered following the Allied liberation of Rome in June 1944. Field Marshal Albert Kesselring, commander of German forces in Italy, denied that he sanctioned or was directly involved in the massacre during his 1947 trial. His conviction and death sentence for other war crimes was commuted to life in prison, and he was released in 1952. Kappler was convicted in 1948 by an Italian military tribunal and sentenced to life in prison. He managed to escape to West Germany in 1977, where he died of cancer the following year at age 70.

Herbert Kappler was tried and convicted in Italy in 1948. (Public Domain Government of Italy via Wikimedia Commons)

RAF RAID ON NUREMBERG

Initial weather reports indicated that cloud cover would offer some protection but the skies above the target would be clear. However, the perspective changed in the hours leading up to this night's Royal Air Force raid on Nuremberg, a centre of German armaments manufacture, and symbolically a city steeped in the rise of Nazi fervour throughout the country as home to the mass party rallies of the 1930s.

RAF Bomber Command was aware of the changing weather conditions but declined to call the raid off, and to make matters more daunting a full moon rose, providing ideal atmospheric circumstances for Luftwaffe night fighters. In the event the RAF lost more airmen in a single night than in the entire Battle of Britain four years earlier.

The Nuremberg raid was given priority in strength with 820 heavy bombers, Avro Lancasters and Handley Page Halifaxes of No. 1, 3, 4, 5, 6, and 8 Groups. Fifteen De Havilland Mosquito fighters were assigned to fly escort to help ward off attacks from the enemy night fighters. Around 10pm, the bombers lifted off from their various airfields and formed up for the flight to the target, crossing the North Sea and the Belgian coastline.

The onslaught of Luftwaffe aircraft began over Belgium, and Flight Lieutenant Neville Sparks, flying a Lancaster of No. 83 Squadron, Pathfinder Force, described the unfolding debacle: "We saw sparkles of cannon fire, some distant and some almost directly above us, followed by explosions, fires, plunging planes, and a scattering of fires on the ground as far as the eye could see. My navigator, 'Doc' Watson, marked no less than 57 ticks on the way to the target. Each tick was a four-engined bomber we'd seen shot down by German fighters…It was the most terrible thing I have ever seen."

During the run-in to the target, 82 RAF heavy bombers were shot down, nearly all of them by Luftwaffe night fighters. On the return leg, 14 more were lost, and among those that returned to their bases another

RAF Avro Lancaster heavy bombers fly over Britain. These four-engine aircraft devastated German cities and military targets during World War Two. (Public Domain collections of the Imperial War Museums via Wikimedia Commons)

Above: The ruins of Nuremberg after many RAF and US Army Air Forces bombing raids are shown in 1945. (Public Domain US Army via Wikimedia Commons)

Left: The silhouette of an RAF Handley Page Halifax bomber crosses a target during a bombing raid on Nazi-occupied Europe. (Public Domain collections of the Imperial War Museums via Wikimedia Commons)

10 were written off as too heavily damaged for further operations. In all, 106 bombers were lost along with more than 700 airmen, including 545 killed and 160 taken prisoner. Assessments of the damage were disappointing, indicating that the industrial facilities, including the MAN works that produced a variety of weapons and components, the Siemens factories that built electric motors, parts for mines, and searchlights, and other engineering locations were minimally impacted.

Twenty-two-year-old Pilot Officer Cyril 'Cy' Barton, piloting a Halifax bomber nicknamed *Excalibur* on his 19th mission, received a posthumous Victoria Cross for remaining at the controls of his stricken aircraft, then flying on only one engine and unable to reach the field at RAF Burn in North Yorkshire, until crash landing in County Durham. Three crewmen survived.

DE GAULLE TAKES COMMAND OF FREE FRENCH FORCES

On April 4, 1944 General Charles de Gaulle, for many the embodiment of the true government of France during the years of Nazi occupation and the guardian of its national honour, took sole command of Free French forces fighting the Nazis.

Following the Allied victory in North Africa, de Gaulle and General Henri Giraud had agreed to serve as joint presidents of the French Committee of National Liberation, formed in Algeria in June 1943. However, the politically astute de Gaulle outmanoeuvred Giraud to gain the lion's share of popular support. Giraud resigned in the spring of 1944, leaving de Gaulle as the de facto leader of the Free French forces, which had grown substantially in size since the dark days of 1940 when the German military juggernaut conquered the country, occupying much of the north and coastal areas while establishing a puppet government in the city of Vichy in the south.

Amid the collapse of the French nation and the capitulation of its armed forces in 1940, de Gaulle escaped to Great Britain and issued a historic BBC radio broadcast, imploring French citizens to rally to him. The appeal of June 18 resonated with those opposing the Nazis or national collaboration with them. The leader declared: "I, General de Gaulle, who is currently in London, invite the French officers and soldiers who are on British territory or who may find themselves there, with or without their weapons, I invite the engineers and workers specialising in the armaments industries who are on British territory or who may find themselves there, to get in touch with me. Whatever happens, the flame of French resistance must not be extinguished and will not be extinguished…."

Meanwhile, de Gaulle's former mentor and benefactor, World War One hero

Charles de Gaulle (right) and Henri Giraud shake hands during their historic meeting in Casablanca in 1943. (Public Domain Frank Capra Divide and Conquer US Government via Wikimedia Commons)

Left: Charles de Gaulle became the leader of the Free French forces during the course of World War Two. (Public Domain United States Government via Wikimedia Commons)

Below: General Charles de Gaulle and King George VI inspect Free French troops in Britain in 1940. (Public Domain collections of the Imperial War Museums via Wikimedia Commons)

Marshal Philippe Petain, was installed as head of the collaborationist Vichy government, and de Gaulle was tried and convicted of treason in absentia and sentenced to death. However, the once obscure brigadier was undeterred, asserting his authority and rallying the French people to fight the Nazis. His representative Jean Moulin worked to unify the various anti-Nazi resistance groups operating in occupied France under de Gaulle's authority as well. Through the remainder of World War Two, de Gaulle struggled to maintain French influence and status among the Allied nations, resulting in substantial friction in relations with US President Franklin D. Roosevelt and British Prime Minister Winston Churchill.

By the time de Gaulle assumed sole command of Free French forces, more than 100,000 French troops had already fought in the Italian campaign in 1943. By D-Day, June 6, 1944, the Free French forces numbered more than 300,000.

BADOGLIO GOVERNMENT FALLS AND REFORMS

On April 21, Italian Prime Minister Pietro Badoglio formed a new government immediately after his first had fallen under pressure from several political factions within the country, particularly its communist elements.

A senior military commander during World War One, Badoglio at first opposed the fascist government of Benito Mussolini, but later became a prime mover of Italian military involvement in Libya, during the invasion of Ethiopia in the mid-1930s, and then Italian adventurism during World War Two, serving as army chief of staff from 1925 to 1940. Following numerous military setbacks, the fascist Grand Council removed Mussolini from office in July 1943, and King Victor Emmanuel III prevailed upon Badoglio to serve as prime minister and form a new government.

A political sycophant, Badoglio accepted the job and negotiated an armistice with the Allies on the eve of their invasion of the Italian mainland in September 1943. Wary of the probable intervention of Nazi forces should the armistice be made public, Badoglio wavered in announcing the agreement. However, US General Dwight Eisenhower, commander of Allied forces in the Mediterranean theatre, did publicly announce the surrender of Italy on September 8, one day before Allied forces hit the beaches at Salerno in the south of the country.

Above: Allied forces land at Salerno on the Italian mainland in September 1943. (Public Domain US Navy via Wikimedia Commons)

Right: Marshal Pietro Badoglio became Prime Minister of Italy with the ouster of Benito Mussolini. (Public Domain Government of Italy via Wikimedia Commons)

Badoglio gave no instruction to the Italian Army, and German forces quickly occupied the country. Fearing arrest by the Germans, Badoglio and King Victor Emmanuel fled Rome for Brindisi, which became the new seat of the Italian government. As part of the surrender agreement, Italy formally changed sides in October 1943, joining the Allies in the fight against Nazi Germany.

The first Badoglio government was unstable from the beginning, due primarily to the threat of German occupation, the prime minister's own history of political opportunism, and his implication in war crimes. Badoglio had been responsible for atrocities committed against opposing forces in Libya decades earlier, as well as during the war of conquest in Ethiopia. Many prisoners had died of starvation in concentration camps while Badoglio had also sanctioned the use of poison gas in the conflict.

During the turbulent period of the first Badoglio government, anti-fascist political groups and those opposed to the continuation of the monarchy were active in their campaign to share power while pressure from the communists increased. With the stability of the first government in jeopardy after 273 days, Badoglio announced the new coalition with the Committee of National Liberation (CLN), formed by six factions – the Italian Communist Party, Italian Socialist Party, Action Party, Christian Democratic Party, Labour Democratic Party, and Italian Liberal Party.

The first Italian government to include socialists and communists, Badoglio's coalition survived for 57 days before it became clear that a change was required. He resigned on June 9, 1944, yielding to a new regime under Ivanoe Bonomi of the Labour Democratic Party.

Marshal Pietro Badoglio (far left) is shown during the Italian military aggression in Ethiopia. (Public Domain Republic of Poland via Wikimedia Commons)

US FORCES LAND AT HOLLANDIA AND AITAPE IN NEW GUINEA

Taking the Japanese completely by surprise, US troops of the 24th, 32nd, and 41st Infantry Divisions landed at Hollandia and Aitape on the northern coast of the island of New Guinea. Operation Reckless was the execution of General Douglas MacArthur's continuing advance in New Guinea in preparation for his much-anticipated return to the Philippines, under Japanese occupation since 1942.

MacArthur had modified his original plan to continue the combined US-Australian offensive against the Japanese in New Guinea with attacks on enemy strongholds at Wewak and Hansa Bay. Instead, he chose to leapfrog those positions and land at Hollandia and Aitape, centrally located on New Guinea's northern coast. MacArthur reasoned that Japanese resistance would be lighter while the airfields at Hollandia along with the fine harbour at adjacent Humboldt Bay would serve as excellent staging areas when his forces later turned north toward the Philippines. In concert with the Hollandia operation, Aitape village, 125 miles southeast, and its nearby airfields were to be seized.

Prior to the landings, fighter sweeps by General George Kenney's Fifth Air Force decimated Japanese air power in New Guinea, destroying more than 300 enemy planes between March 30 and April 3. Naval bombardment preceded the Hollandia landings on April 22, as the bulk of the 41st Division came ashore on two beaches at Humboldt Bay and the 24th landed 22 miles west at Tanahmerah Bay. Meanwhile, the 163rd Infantry Regiment, detached from the 41st Division, and the 127th Infantry Regiment, 32nd Division came ashore at Aitape with fire support from cruisers and destroyers of the Australian and US Navies.

Beachheads were rapidly consolidated at Hollandia as the Japanese were observed generally abandoning defensive positions. At Humboldt Bay, only six Americans were killed and 16 wounded on the first day. Hollandia town was taken without a fight on April 23. Three days

US landing craft and LSTs (Landing Ship, Tank) are shown ashore at Hollandia, New Guinea, April 22, 1944. (Public Domain US Navy via Wikimedia Commons)

US soldiers advance into the jungle from their landing point at Tanahmerah Bay, Hollandia, New Guinea. (Public Domain US Army via Wikimedia Commons)

later, all three airfields at Hollandia were in US hands. Although the Americans had expected heavy fighting on several occasions, the Japanese declined and withdrew. A similar situation unfolded at Aitape, which fell to US troops in three days.

The bulk of Japanese forces retired toward Sarmi and Wakde some 125 miles west, but the harsh jungle conditions, lack of food, and debilitating tropical diseases took a heavy toll. Only a fraction of those Japanese soldiers, numbering more than 7,000, actually reached safety. All American objectives at Hollandia had been achieved by April 27, and the area was declared secure in early June. A Japanese force of 20,000 troops attacked the Americans at Aitape on June 28, and fighting in the vicinity persisted until August.

Allied forces suffered fewer than 200 killed during Operation Reckless, while Japanese casualties topped 4,000 dead, wounded, or taken prisoner. As MacArthur envisioned, Hollandia soon became a major supply base for future offensive operations in the Philippines.

A US Navy Douglas SBD Dauntless dive bomber flies over Tanahmerah Bay, Hollandia, as landing craft approach the shore. (Public Domain US Navy via Wikimedia Commons)

EXERCISE TIGER: SLAPTON SANDS TRAGEDY

Off Slapton Sands on the coast of Devon between the port towns of Brixham and Salcombe, swift German E-boats, heavily armed with guns and torpedoes, surprised a flotilla of eight US LSTs (Landing Ship, Tank), wreaking havoc among the virtually defenceless craft. Exercise Tiger, a simulated amphibious landing in preparation for the D-Day invasion of French Normandy, was thrown into confusion. When the Germans departed, 749 dead American soldiers and sailors were left in their wake, while two LSTs were sunk and two others badly damaged.

During the Allied buildup of troops and supplies prior to D-Day, the US 4th Infantry Division had been assigned to a training centre on the Devon coast, a 25-square-mile area where landing tactics and interservice cooperation were to be perfected. Training exercises were common in the early months of 1944, and one of the largest involved the 23,000 soldiers of the 4th Division, under the command of General Raymond O. 'Tubby' Barton.

The LSTs were versatile transport craft, capable of holding 300 infantrymen and 60 vehicles and delivering them right onto the beach, their massive bow doors swinging open to disgorge their cargoes. They were 322ft long and somewhat ponderous, typically armed with only 20mm and 40mm anti-aircraft guns and light or heavy machine guns.

Exercise Tiger got underway with some difficulty on April 26, 1944. An order delaying H-Hour by 60 minutes was never received by some units of the 4th Division, while communications at sea were snarled when the LSTs and their escorting Royal Navy destroyers were assigned different radio frequencies and were unable to communicate. The destroyer HMS *Scimitar* sustained minor damage during a nocturnal collision and was forced to return to Plymouth temporarily. However, when *Scimitar* returned to take up her station, she was ordered away, leaving the rear of the flotilla unprotected. Only the destroyer HMS *Saladin* and the corvette HMS *Azalea* remained to protect the vulnerable LSTs.

Hundreds of American soldiers had embarked aboard the LSTs, which were nicknamed 'Large Slow Targets', and at dawn on April 27 the first wave was put ashore amid simulated machine-gun and artillery fire. Fake dead bodies had been strewn along the beach to add to the realism. The initial wave, however, was marked with confusion. Some landing craft veered into incorrect zones. Others became piled up in

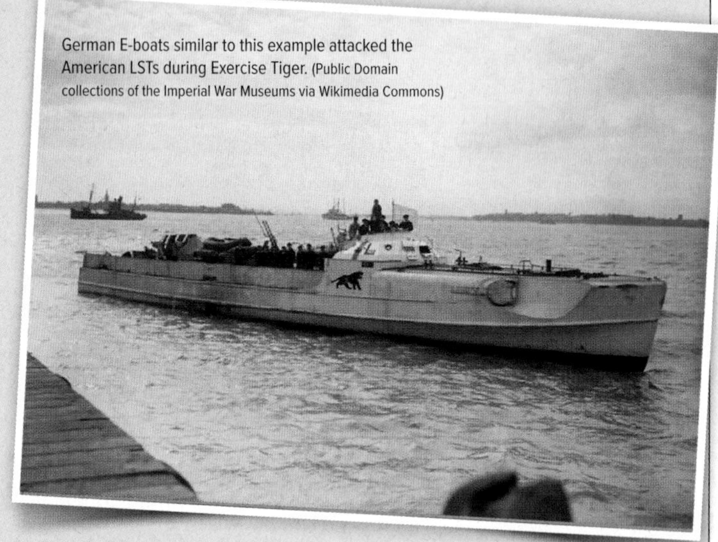

German E-boats similar to this example attacked the American LSTs during Exercise Tiger. (Public Domain collections of the Imperial War Museums via Wikimedia Commons)

traffic jams, finally coming ashore in the wrong places. There were too few naval officers available to make order of the chaos. However, Exercise Tiger proceeded as the troops of the second and third waves were waiting offshore along with their tanks and other heavy equipment.

By the evening of April 27, the LSTs were churning through Lyme Bay on course toward Slapton Sands about 40 miles distant. The second and third waves were to go ashore with daylight; however, at 2am, about 15 miles off Portland Bill, the calm was shattered when nine E-boats, patrolling from their base at Cherbourg, sliced into the unsuspecting landing ships. Painted black, the attackers were nearly indistinguishable in the darkness, but the tracer rounds from their guns glowed an eerie green and struck home savagely.

LST-*507* was hit by a pair of torpedoes and erupted in a sheet of flame. Gasoline ruptured from the tanks of US Army trucks aboard, spilling into the inferno and adding to the conflagration as it poured over the side and mixed with fuel oil haemorrhaging from the bunkers of the wounded vessel, which soon sank.

American soldiers come ashore at Slapton Sands during training exercises prior to D-Day. (Public Domain US Army via Wikimedia Commons)

An amphibious DUKW vehicle and crane are shown unloading supplies on the beach at Slapton Sands. (Public Domain US Government via Wikimedia Commons)

A US tank destroyer comes ashore at Slapton Sands while an LST has reached the beach in the background. (Creative Commons PhotosNormandie via Wikimedia Commons)

Minutes later, two more torpedoes slammed into LST-*531*, and an eyewitness watched "a gigantic orange-ball explosion, like something from the movies, a flame like it had come from hell, with little black specks round the edges which we knew were Jeeps or boat stanchions, or men." LST-*531* sank even more quickly than LST-*507*. Meanwhile, gunners aboard the landing ships began firing wildly into the night. Some of these rounds mistakenly struck LST-*511* as a targeted E-boat sped across an American's field of vision.

Pictured off Omaha Beach on D-Day, LST-511 was damaged by German E-boats during Exercise Tiger. (Public Domain US Navy via Wikimedia Commons)

Soldiers and sailors foundered in the roiling water, some of them on fire and others drowning under the burden of their kit or suffering from shock and hypothermia. Half an hour after the first shots had been fired, another German torpedo nearly blew the stern off LST-*289*. Luckily, its crew managed to keep the damaged vessel afloat.

Due to an order to maintain radio silence, word of the unfolding debacle spread slowly, and by the time the destroyer HMS *Onslow* had led a small task group to the scene, the enemy E-boats had sped away. The remaining six LSTs limped back into port even as the damage and loss of life were being assessed. The early death toll stood at 639, but this was revised upward by 110 as the missing were accounted for. Exercise Tiger, a dress rehearsal for the Normandy landings of Operation Overlord, had become the costliest wartime training disaster in US military history.

In the aftermath of the tragedy, General Dwight D. Eisenhower, Allied supreme commander, ordered the entire episode to remain secret to preserve morale and avoid compromising Operation Overlord. Survivors were sequestered, and medical personnel that had treated the wounded were warned to say nothing. Fears that the Germans had scored an intelligence coup by capturing individuals who possessed top secret knowledge of the D-Day plans were allayed when all 10 were confirmed as dead.

Reports of the Slapton Sands incident were released after the D-Day landings, and there were accusations of a cover-up. However, the event slipped into obscurity for decades afterward.

This Sherman tank was recovered from the waters off Slapton Sands and dedicated as a memorial to those lost during Exercise Tiger. (Copyrighted Free Use Link Shahirshamsir via Wikimedia Commons)

B-24 LIBERATOR PRODUCTION PEAKS AT WILLOW RUN

Workers at Willow Run install an engine in a Consolidated B-24 Liberator heavy bomber. (Public Domain FDR Presidential Library National Archives and Records Administration via Wikimedia Commons)

A Consolidated B-24 Liberator heavy bomber flies through smoke and enemy flak at Ploesti, August 1, 1943. (Public Domain US Army Center of Military History via Wikimedia Commons)

On April 30, 1944, monthly production of the four-engine Consolidated B-24 Liberator heavy bomber peaked at 428 at the Willow Run assembly plant 30 miles west of Detroit, Michigan.

The Liberator was produced in greater numbers than any other American military aircraft of World War Two and served in all theatres. By the end of 1943, there were 550 Liberators serving in Europe, and more than 45 US Army Air Forces bomber groups flew the plane during the conflict. A total of 19,203 Liberators were built in US factories by 1945, and with war's end orders for another 5,168 were cancelled.

The Liberator was flown during many high-profile missions during the air war in Europe, including Operation Tidal Wave, the August 1, 1943, bombing of the oil refining facilities at Ploesti, Romania. With a crew of up to 10 airmen, the bomber was 67ft long with a wingspan of 110ft, cruising speed of 290mph, and payload of up to 12,800lb, actually exceeding that of the contemporary Boeing B-17 Flying Fortress. The B-24 was constructed of 1,225,000 parts held together with 313,237 rivets at a cost of $187,000 per plane.

A US Army Air Forces training manual offered: "The B-24, when properly used, has no equal in any air force. It has proved itself capable of delivering tremendous blows against the enemy over long ranges, under favourable weather conditions and against heavy enemy opposition…."

The supply of B-24 Liberators was significantly augmented when the controversial Willow Run plant came on line. Henry Ford, chairman of Ford Motor Company, had pioneered mass production techniques, and by 1941 it was clear that the Liberator had to be produced in greater numbers. The project was turned over to his son, Edsel, and Ford production wizard Charles Sorensen. Designer Albert Kahn was tasked with developing blueprints for the big factory, and he promised to deliver "the most enormous room in the history of man." Construction began on April 18, 1941, and on completion the facility stretched 3,200ft

in length and was 1,279ft wide at its widest point. The assembly line alone stretched half a mile. During the course of the war, B-24 design modifications were continual, and Willow Run adapted.

Sceptics watched the construction of the mammoth facility along the way, and when delays were encountered, some posed the rhetorical question: "Will it run?" In fact, it did. The first Liberator was completed at the sprawling Michigan plant on May 15, 1942.

Before the Willow Run facility closed in 1945, it had produced 8,685 B-24 bombers using 3.5m sq ft of factory floor space. Its peak monthly production of was reached at a time when Ford was producing 70 percent of all B-24s, one rolling off the assembly line every 51 minutes.

As far as the eye can see, B-24 Liberator bombers proceed down the assembly line at Ford's Willow Run manufacturing facility. (Public Domain United States Farm Security Administration via Wikimedia Commons)

STATE OF THE WAR JANUARY-APRIL 1944

On January 11, 1944, President Franklin D. Roosevelt came before a joint session of the US Congress to deliver the annual State of the Union Address. The United States and its allies were in the midst of the great World War Two. While America had been officially fighting for just over two years, Great Britain had been in armed conflict for more than four, and the Soviet Union since the summer of 1941 when the duplicitous Nazis had violated a 1939 non-aggression pact and unleashed their massive war machine in a ruthless quest for "lebensraum," or living space, in the east.

During desperate fighting from the Russian steppes to the desert of North Africa, from the deep of the Atlantic Ocean to the vastness of the Pacific, from the jungles of Asia to the contested islands that marked the bloody slog toward Japan, hard-won victories had turned the prospect of outright and total defeat into a perspective on victory. As Roosevelt had declared the day after the Japanese attack on Pearl

Left: President Franklin D. Roosevelt warned against complacency in the State of the Union Address of 1944. (Creative Commons FDR Presidential Library and Museum via Wikimedia Commons)

Right: German Field Marshal Friedrich Paulus surrenders the Sixth Army at Stalingrad. (Creative Commons Bundesarchiv Bild via Wikimedia Commons)

Below: German and Italian prisoners are gathered for disposition in Tunisia in the spring of 1943. (Public Domain collections of the Imperial War Museums via Wikimedia Commons)

Harbor: "No matter how long it may take us…" the Allies had seized the initiative. The turning points of 1942 at Midway and El Alamein had marked, as Prime Minister Winston Churchill so eloquently uttered, "…the end of the beginning."

In the same pivotal year, RAF Bomber Command and the US Army Air Forces began a sustained and devastating bombing campaign against Nazi Germany, meting out retribution for the destruction sown by Luftwaffe planes in the dark early days of the war. They carried out the pronouncement of Marshal of the Royal Air Force Sir Arthur 'Bomber' Harris, leader of RAF Bomber Command, who proclaimed: "The Nazis entered this war under the rather childish delusion that they were going to bomb everybody else, and nobody was going to bomb them…They sowed the wind and now they are going to reap the whirlwind…It may take a year. It may take two…There is a great deal of work to be done first and let us all get down to it."

Through 1943, the Axis enemy had been ejected thoroughly from the African continent, then pushed out of Sicily and forced on the defensive as Allied armies slugged their way up the boot of the Italian mainland. The Soviets had won perhaps the greatest single victory of the fight against the Nazis at Stalingrad, where the German Sixth Army was utterly destroyed, and Red Army troops and tanks had prevailed in the great armoured clash at Kursk. The Japanese had been defeated at Guadalcanal and Tarawa and elsewhere in the Pacific and placed squarely on the defensive as the US made a remarkable recovery from the Pearl Harbor disaster and struck back hard.

Still, there would be much fighting and terrible sacrifice required before final Allied victory could be achieved.

As he spoke, President Roosevelt acknowledged the rising tide of Allied triumphs in early 1944, but that nod came with a stark warning. "If ever there was a time to subordinate individual or group selfishness to the national good, that time is now," he stated. "Disunity at home – bickerings, self-seeking partisanship, stoppages of work, inflation, business as usual, politics as usual, luxury as usual, these are the influences which can undermine the morale of the brave men ready to die at the front for us here."

The President went on to further admonish those whose activities diminished the drive toward victory, even if unaware that they were doing so. "Those who are doing most of the complaining are not deliberately striving to sabotage the national war effort," he explained. "They are laboring under the delusion that the time is past when we must make prodigious sacrifices – that the war is already won, and we can begin to slacken off. But the dangerous folly of that point of view can be measured by the distance that separates our troops from their ultimate objectives in Berlin and Tokyo – and by the sum of all the perils that lie along the way."

And then, FDR drove home his salient point. "Overconfidence and complacency are among our deadliest enemies. Last spring, after notable victories at Stalingrad and in Tunisia and against the U-boats on the high seas – overconfidence became so pronounced that war production fell off. In two months, June, and July, 1943, more than a thousand airplanes that could have been made and should have been made were not made. Those who failed to make them were not on strike. They were merely saying, 'The war's in the bag – so let's relax.' That attitude on the part of anyone – government or management or labor – can lengthen this war. It can kill American boys…."

The same observation would hold true for British boys, Soviet boys, French boys, and so on. Perhaps the most frightful prospect of all in the early days and weeks of 1944 was any weakening of the resolve that had brought the Allied cause to this point of progress.

Regardless of the risk of public complacency at home, there were no such illusions among the highest echelons of the Allied military.

Above: Allied forces come ashore in Sicily in the summer of 1943, carrying the war to Axis territory. (Public Domain collections if the Imperial War Museums via Wikimedia Commons)

Left: Prime Minister Winston Churchill tours facilities in Britain during the buildup of supplies and weapons for D-Day. (Public Domain US Army via Wikimedia Commons)

Soviet defenders of Leningrad gather during a lull in the fighting. The 900-day siege of the city was lifted in early 1944. (Public Domain RIA Novosti via Wikimedia Commons)

US landing craft are shown approaching the coast of New Guinea at Hollandia in early 1944. (Public Domain US Department of Defense via Wikimedia Commons)

Battles were being fought, costly battles, many of them won but some lost or indecisive in outcome. Plans were in the works.

The buildup of American and Allied forces in Britain in anticipation of the cross-Channel attack on Hitler's Fortress Europe proceeded apace. General Dwight Eisenhower and SHAEF (Supreme Headquarters Allied Expeditionary Force) worked feverishly to solve the myriad of challenges associated with Operation Overlord, not only in gaining a foothold on the continent, but in sustaining the war in the West in its drive toward the German frontier. Meanwhile, the bloody fighting in Italy seemed as though it might never end. Casualties were frightful, and even as the main route of advance had stalled at the formidable Gustav Line south of Rome, the amphibious landings at Anzio had not produced the immediate results envisioned to outflank the German defences and open the road to Rome.

The air war in Europe proceeded as the RAF bombed by night and the US Eighth and Fifteenth Air Forces resumed daylight attacks with the Big Week campaign in February. Eighth Air Force daylight raids had been temporarily suspended after horrendous losses in heavy bombers during the autumn of 1943.

On the Eastern Front, the Red Army followed the victory at Stalingrad with offensive operations that lifted the 900-day siege of Leningrad and then proceeded to push German Army Group North significantly westward. During their winter offensive in Ukraine, two Red Army fronts under the command of Marshal Ivan Konev and General Nikolai Vatutin encircled two corps of German Army Group South in the Cherkassy pocket and inflicted massive casualties before the enemy forces were able to break out of the trap.

In the Pacific, General Douglas MacArthur and his US and Australian forces continued to fight the Japanese in New Guinea, while key locations in the Admiralties group were seized to facilitate the isolation of the Japanese bastion of Rabaul on the island of New Britain and the progress toward eventual landings to wrest control of the Philippines from the enemy. Seeadler Harbor on the island of Manus was destined to play a key role in the Allied advance toward Japan. In the early months of 1944, American forces captured the island of Kwajalein in the Marshalls archipelago, while carrier-based aircraft devastated the big Japanese base at Truk in the Carolines.

In the China-Burma-India theatre, Brigadier Orde Wingate's Chindits and Merrill's Marauders made history fighting behind the Japanese lines in Burma, while General William Slim and the British and Commonwealth troops of his 14th Army won major victories at the pivotal battles of Imphal and Kohima to turn back a Japanese offensive intended to conquer India.

As Allied leaders acknowledged, there were triumphs to celebrate and sacrifices that inspired. But everywhere the Axis enemy remained a potent adversary, ideologically charged and willing to fight and die for his cause no matter how dastardly. Although progress toward final Allied victory had been achieved, there were more perilous days to come in 1944.

Above: US troops come ashore in the Admiralty Islands at Los Negros in February 1944. (Public Domain US Army via Wikimedia Commons)

Below: British troops approach the Italian mainland at Taranto during the Allied invasion of September 1943. (Public Domain collections of the Imperial War Museums via Wikimedia Commons)

SOVIET FORCES LIBERATE SEVASTOPOL

Seizing the initiative following the great victory at Stalingrad, the Soviet Red Army launched offensive actions along the Eastern Front. In the south, the Crimean Offensive culminated with the liberation of Sevastopol, a key port on the coast of the Crimean Peninsula and once home to the Soviet Black Sea Fleet.

Sevastopol had been occupied by the Nazis since the city fell to General Eric von Manstein's Eleventh Army on July 4, 1942, after a 250-day siege. However, by the autumn of 1943, Red Army attacks had forced the Germans to withdraw from their bridgehead across the Kerch Strait connecting the Black Sea and the Sea of Azov to the northeast. The German 17th Army, a component of Army Group South Ukraine, abandoned its positions at Kuban in the north Caucasus, crossing the Perkop Isthmus and retiring into the Crimean Peninsula.

Thousands of German and Romanian troops were essentially bottled up, and STAVKA, the Soviet command, was content to maintain the status quo for the next five months while the Axis forces were supplied by convoys across the Black Sea. Then, in early April 1944, the Red Army's 4th Ukrainian Front, commanded by Marshal Fyodor Tolbukhin, launched the decisive offensive in the Crimea, crossing the Perkop Isthmus and engaging the 17th Army. The 51st and 2nd Guards Armies of the 4th Ukrainian Front advanced swiftly, reaching Simferopol, just 37 miles northeast of Sevastopol within three days.

The Romanian destroyer Regele Ferdinand is shown during the evacuation of Axis forces from Sevastopol in the Crimea. (Public Domain Government of Romania via Wikimedia Commons)

Left: Marshal Fyodor Tolbukhin led the 4th Ukrainian Front in the battle for Sevastopol. (Creative Commons Mil.ru Government of the Russian Federation via Wikimedia Commons)

Below: Red Army soldiers advance in the Crimea during the drive toward Sevastopol. (Public Domain V. Ivanov Russian Federation via Wikimedia Commons)

During the last week of April, the remaining German and Romanian forces had been pushed into a pocket around Sevastopol, which the German high command, Oberkommando des Heeres (OKH), intended to defend in a prolonged standoff if necessary. Actually, the fortifications surrounding Sevastopol had been seriously degraded during the long siege of 1941-1942, handicapping the planned Axis defence of the city. Red Army forces advanced to the outskirts of Sevastopol by the end of the month, and fighting erupted in the streets. After nine days, the German and Romanian troops surrendered.

During the final stages of the battle for Sevastopol, the Germans and Romanians coordinated an evacuation effort that transported nearly 115,000 soldiers to safety, many of them ferried across the Black Sea to the Romanian city of Constanta. Casualties were heavy on both sides with the Germans and Romanians sustaining nearly 100,000 killed, wounded or captured, and the Soviets losing nearly 85,000 soldiers.

In May 1945, Soviet Premier Josef Stalin designated Sevastopol a hero city along with Leningrad, Stalingrad, and Odessa.

OPERATION DIADEM: CRACKING THE GUSTAV LINE

At 11pm on May 11, 1944, more than 1,600 Allied guns of the Fifth and Eighth Armies thundered in the opening phase of Operation Diadem, the final major offensive that succeeded in rupturing the formidable German defences of the Gustav Line, south of Rome. After weeks of stalemate on the Italian front, the Fifth Army was stalled at Cassino, the Eighth Army at Ortona, and VI Corps defending the lodgement at Anzio. Field Marshal Sir Harold Alexander, commander of the Allied 15th Army Group, altered the previous narrow frontal tactics and devised a broad assault, combined with a breakout from the Anzio beachhead, that is expected to unhinge the German defences of the Gustav Line and open the road to Rome.

Most recently, eight days of fighting at the town of Cassino and the third attempt to capture the abbey of Monte Cassino had led to frustration for the Fifth Army. The 4th Indian Division had advanced within 250 yards of the ruined abbey only to be stopped cold by German defenders, while 2,000 Allied soldiers had been killed or wounded and 600,000 artillery shells and bombs expended.

Alexander's Diadem plan called for attacks at four separate locations along the Gustav Line. From left to right the US 85th and

A Polish soldier plays the bugle outside the ruins of the Abbey of Monte Cassino. (Public Domain Government of Poland via Wikimedia Commons)

88th Divisions would advance along Highway 7 up the coast while four divisions of the French Expeditionary Corps trekked through the Aurunci Mountains left of the valley of the River Liri. Three British, two Canadian, and one Indian division with the support of a Canadian armoured brigade were to cross the River Rapido in the centre, and on the right the capture of Monte Cassino was tasked to the Polish II Corps, capably led by General Wladyslaw Anders and 50,000 strong. The 6th South African Armoured Division would be held in reserve. The concurrent VI Corps breakthrough at Anzio would provide an opportunity to trap the retreating German forces south of Rome.

Field Marshal Albert Kesselring, commanding Axis troops in the Mediterranean theatre, was aware that another Allied offensive was coming. During the lull that preceded Diadem, his troops had been busy preparing defensive positions at the Caesar Line near Anzio and the Hitler Line, 10 miles north of the Gustav Line.

Two hours after the artillery bombardment of May 11, the entire Allied offensive surged forward. Two Polish divisions, the 3rd Carpathian and 5th Kresowa, made good initial progress but sustained heavy casualties and were compelled to fall back to their start line the next day. Within hours, though, the British 78th Division attacked along Highway 6, and the Poles launched their second attack along Colle Sant' Angelo Ridge north of the abbey. Quickly, the German 1st Parachute Division was in danger of being cut off at the abbey and finally withdrew. On the morning of May 18, a patrol of the Podolski

Field Marshal Sir Harold Alexander, commander of Allied 15th Army Group, stands before a map of Italy. (Public Domain collections of the Imperial War Museums via Wikimedia Commons)

A tough Moroccan soldier sharpens his bayonet prior to Operation Diadem. The Moroccans, known as Goumiers, fought with the French Expeditionary Force in Italy. (Public Domain US Army via Wikimedia Commons)

Soldiers of the Royal West Kent Regiment, 78th Division man a dugout position near Cassino in March 1944. (Public Domain collections of the Imperial War Museums via Wikimedia Commons)

Lancers at long last occupied the ruins of the abbey of Monte Cassino, capturing 30 wounded enemy soldiers and the medical personnel that had been left behind to tend them.

Meanwhile, the British 4th and Indian 8th Divisions forced a crossing of the Rapido while the US 350th and 351st Infantry Regiments encountered stiff enemy resistance around the town of Santa Maria Infante. Only limited gains were made in both the British/Commonwealth and American attacks. Therefore, the first 24 hours of Operation Diadem were disappointing.

General Alphonse Juin led the French Expeditionary Corps forward through the mountains, his colonial troops from Algeria and Morocco quite familiar with such difficult terrain. The 2nd Moroccan Division fought ferociously against the German 71st Division, eventually capturing 150 prisoners around Monte Majo by the early morning of May 13. Supported by heavy artillery fire, the Moroccans continued their advance, opening the flank of the XIV Panzer Korps to attack. At the same time, the British managed to expand their bridgehead across the Rapido to 2,500 yards and the American divisions found resistance to their renewed advances quite diminished with only sporadic small-arms fire to their front.

By May 14, Santa Maria Infante had fallen, and the Americans had captured a key road junction along Highway 7, outflanking its German defenders. The French advance toward the Liri Valley impeded Kesselring's efforts to reinforce his endangered positions, and the Gustav Line was finally abandoned. Alexander exhorted the advance, hoping to breach the Hitler Line before it could be occupied in strength. These operations met stiff opposition in some areas but were successful. On May 23, the VI Corps breakout from the Anzio beachhead commenced.

Two days later, the implications of the Allied advances were clear to General Heinrich von Vietinghoff, commander of the German Tenth Army. The US II Corps was positioned to rapidly advance up Highway 7 toward the Anzio breakout, while elements of the British Eighth Army were through the Hitler Line and into the Liri Valley that stretched toward Rome. The French, after rupturing the Gustav Line, were threatening to encircle both the Tenth and Fourteenth Armies and to split these forces in two. Vietinghoff ordered a general withdrawal of German forces from southern Italy.

In the coming days, the spearheads of the Fifth and Eighth Armies continued to advance, and the linkup with VI Corps was achieved. In the midst of victory, however, controversy loomed.

A soldier of the US 85th Infantry Division examines an 88mm gun abandoned by the Germans during Operation Diadem in May 1944. (Public Domain US Army Signal Corps Archive via Wikimedia Commons)

Polish soldiers are shown inside the Abbey of Monte Cassino after the ruins were captured during Operation Diadem. (Public Domain Government of Poland via Wikimedia Commons)

MERRILL'S MARAUDERS TAKE MYITKYINA AIRFIELD

Despite their ranks already dangerously depleted after weeks of jungle warfare behind Japanese lines in Burma, soldiers of the 5307th Composite Unit (Provisional), designated Galahad Force but better known as Merrill's Marauders, executed a surprise assault against the Japanese garrison guarding the airfield at Myitkyina and captured the vital link in the supply line for Allied forces engaged in the fighting in the China-Burma-India theatre (CBI).

During Operation End Run, the Marauders also seized the ferry terminal at Pamati while the Chinese 150th Infantry Regiment secured the airfield in the rapid movement, forcing the roughly 700 Japanese defenders in the area to take refuge in nearby Myitkyina town. Possession of the airfield substantially shortened the Allied air route of resupply in the CBI and eased the traffic flow along the Ledo Road, which remained under construction.

Named for their commander, General Frank Merrill, the Marauders were formed in late 1943, training with the famed Chindits of Brigadier Orde Wingate after arriving in Bombay, India, on October 31, and moving 125 miles to camp at Delolali. Wingate's ambitious Operation Thursday, undertaken in early March 1944, provided Merrill's Marauders with their first combat deployment. Merrill's command operated jointly with elements of the Chinese Army under the control of American General Joseph 'Vinegar Joe' Stilwell.

A vicious fight with the Japanese 18th Infantry Division proved the mettle of the Marauders during the first week of March as more than 800 enemy troops were killed, wounded or captured during five days of combat near the southern end of Burma's Hukawng Valley. On March 31, General Merrill suffered the second heart attack of his military career, and command of the Marauders fell to his capable executive officer, Lieutenant Colonel Charles Hunter.

Resupplied by air and covering more than 750 miles on foot, the Marauders had suffered more than 700 casualties due to enemy action, jungle diseases such as malaria that ravaged their ranks, and exhaustion amid the oppressive heat. Merrill had hoped that his men might be relieved prior to the fight at Myitkyina, but the capture of the airfield was crucial, and it had to be accomplished before the onset of the

Top: Generals Frank Merrill (left) and Joseph Stilwell confer during operations in Burma. (Public Domain US Army via Wikimedia Commons)

Above: General Joseph Stilwell presents medals to members of Merrill's Marauders at Myitkyina. (Public Domain US Signal Corps Department of Defense via Wikimedia Commons)

Left: Merrill's Marauders take a momentary rest during a long, arduous jungle trek. (Public Domain US Signal Corps Department of Defense via Wikimedia Commons)

monsoon season. By the time the airfield was taken, only about 1,500 Marauders, roughly half their original strength, were physically able to carry a rifle.

At the end of May, the Marauders had spent three months behind enemy lines and fought five extended engagements against the Japanese while coordinating with elements of the Chinese Army. Although reinforcements arrived, the siege of Myitkyina took a further toll. By June only 200 of the original Marauders remained. The 3,500 Japanese troops in the town fought tenaciously until August, when their supply line was severed. The Marauders had lost another 570 soldiers to disease during the siege while 1,244 Allied troops were killed and over 4,000 wounded.

After Myitkyina, Merrill's Marauders ceased to be an effective fighting force, and the unit's survivors were assigned to the 475th Infantry Regiment.

ALLIED VI CORPS, FIFTH ARMY LINK UP AT ANZIO

On May 25, after two days of fighting, the Allied VI Corps linked up with Fifth Army forces from the south during Operation Buffalo, the breakout from the Anzio beachhead. Four months of frustration and agony had come to an end, and VI Corps no longer languished contained by the Germans after landing at Anzio during Operation Shingle on January 22.

General John P. Lucas, commanding VI Corps, had chosen to consolidate his beachhead rather than advancing to the Alban Hills and on toward Rome while outflanking the defences of the Gustav Line, thereby allowing the Germans time to respond to the surprise landings at Anzio. During the weeks that followed, Allied strength in the beachhead increased from two divisions to seven, German efforts to drive the lodgement back into the sea had failed, and stalemate had developed while casualties mounted on both sides.

Lucas was relieved in February, and General Lucian Truscott was elevated from command of the US 3rd Infantry Division to take his place. Meanwhile, plans were developed to end the frustrating situation to the south at Cassino and along the length of the Gustav Line, where stubborn German forces were well-positioned to deny the Allied Fifth and Eighth Armies further advance. After repeated efforts to pierce the enemy fortifications had failed, Field Marshal Sir Harold Alexander, commander of the Allied 15th Army Group, devised Operation Diadem, a broad assault against the Gustav Line to begin in mid-May.

In conjunction with Diadem, Alexander instructed General Mark Clark, commander of the Fifth Army, to prepare for a breakout from the Anzio beachhead. Clark, in turn, ordered Truscott to prepare for one of four options to execute the mission. Operation Buffalo was the choice since it most closely aligned with Field Marshal Alexander's Diadem plan. Buffalo, set to commence 12 days after Diadem, involved a VI Corps thrust to the northeast through the towns of Cisterna and Valmontone, cutting Highway 6 and trapping German forces of the Tenth and Fourteenth Armies to the south.

Rome, the first Axis capital likely to fall to the Allies, was approximately 35 miles northwest of Anzio. But in the Operation Buffalo scenario the Eternal City would become a secondary objective. While Rome had some military significance as a communications and transportation centre, its liberation would be more of a symbolic triumph for the Allies. Conversely, a crippling military blow including the capture of thousands of German soldiers in the south might

Above: British infantrymen of the 1st Battalion, Green Howards occupy a captured German trench on the eve of Operation Buffalo at Anzio. (Public Domain collections of the Imperial War Museums via Wikimedia Commons)

Right: General Lucian Truscott commanded VI Corps during Operation Buffalo, the breakout from the Anzio beachhead. (Public Domain Harris & Ewing Photo Studio Library of Congress via Wikimedia Commons)

shorten World War Two in the Mediterranean considerably and ease the remainder of the long Allied campaign in Italy. Although Alexander appreciated the situation in total, the two proposed axis of advance, toward Rome or further east to cut off the enemy retreat, were 20 miles apart. He did not believe they could be accomplished simultaneously.

Clark, however, disagreed. He saw Rome as the prize and concluded that cutting Highway 6 would do little to deter the retreating Germans. Further, if the linkup with Fifth Army occurred quickly, Truscott might still turn toward Rome. He noted that the Alban Hills should be taken prior to the advance on Valmontone to eliminate any German threat to the VI Corps rear. The Alban Hills were the last natural barrier south of Rome, and it followed that if they were secured then Rome itself should follow. Clark also desperately wanted American forces rather than the British to capture the Italian capital. He believed that the US troops had not been given sufficient credit during the campaign, and the personal glory associated with the city's capture held tremendous appeal. Clark was keenly aware that D-Day, the invasion of northwest Europe, was set for early June. Once Allied forces were ashore in Normandy, the Mediterranean theatre would become a sideshow.

For months, Alexander had made his preference for a drive on Valmontone rather than directly to Rome known to his senior officers,

A German Fallschirmjäger looks skyward as his unit takes up positions at Anzio in May 1944. (Public Domain National Digital Archives of Poland via Wikimedia Commons)

but he did not issue a direct order to Clark. Nevertheless, his intent with Operation Buffalo was clear.

On the night of May 22, the British 1st Division made a diversionary attack along the Anzio-Albano road, and within hours Combat Commands A and B of the US 1st Armored Division launched Operation Buffalo. On the first day, the Americans crossed the rail line to Rome and reached their objective, a low ridge north of the beachhead, driving a mile into the defensive perimeter of the German 362nd Division. The 3rd Infantry Division hit Cisterna at 6:30am and fought for two days before entering the town.

Simultaneously, the US-Canadian First Special Service Force had taken high ground at Monte Arrestino.

Near daybreak on May 25, combat engineers of the US 36th Infantry Division moved

Left: General Mark Clark led the Allied Fifth Army during the Italian Campaign. (Public Domain US Army via Wikimedia Commons)

Right: Soldiers of the 2nd Royal Inniskilling Fusiliers receive a rum ration while a bagpiper plays at Anzio. (Public Domain collections of the Imperial War Museums via Wikimedia Commons)

Below: British and American soldiers meet along a roadway near Anzio during operations in May 1944. (Creative Commons Fidodog14 via Wikimedia Commons)

south from Anzio across the Mussolini Canal, making contact with a task force of the 85th Infantry Division advancing north. After 125 days, the VI Corps was no longer isolated. Now it was the left flank of Fifth Army.

Truscott's VI Corps was poised to continue its advance on Valmontone. However, Rome still glittered in the distance.

OPERATION FRANTIC SHUTTLE BOMBING BEGINS

At the beginning of June, the first of 129 Boeing B-17 Flying Fortress heavy bombers of the US Army Air Forces and their 64 escorting fighter planes landed in unfamiliar territory, the airfield at Poltava in central Ukraine. These aircraft were the vanguard of Operation Frantic, an ambitious but challenging initiative that would allow American bombers and fighters of the Eighth and Fifteenth Air Forces to bomb the Third Reich and other targets in Nazi-occupied Europe, fly on to airfields in the Soviet Union, refuel and re-arm, and then hit enemy targets on the return flights to their bases in England and Italy.

Dubbed Operation Frantic, the shuttle bombing had been months in the making. Despite the fact that the Western Allies and the Soviet Union were cooperating in their fight against Nazi Germany in World War Two, an element of mistrust was still present. In assessing the benefits of Operation Frantic, American air planners asserted that shuttle missions would stretch Luftwaffe air defences to the limit as the bombers raided high-value targets in the days surrounding the D-Day invasion of Western Europe. Targets in Eastern Europe would be more within reach, while the programme itself would foster greater cooperation between the Allied armed forces, perhaps leading to a future agreement in the war against Imperial Japan.

After months of negotiation, the final go-ahead was received after the Tehran Conference of November 1943, and three bases – Poltava, Piryatin, and Mirgorod – each within 50 miles of one another and roughly 450 miles southwest of Moscow were chosen. Poltava was

A Flying Fortress bomber crew pauses for a photograph during Operation Frantic. (Creative Commons National Archives of Ukraine via Wikimedia Commons)

Left: American and Soviet officers and dignitaries meet at Poltava on June 2, 1944. (Public Domain US Air Force via Wikimedia Commons)

Below: A B-17 Flying Fortress lies utterly destroyed at Poltava after the Germain air raid of June 21, 1944. (Public Domain US Air Force via Wikimedia Commons)

designated the headquarters for Operation Frantic, and some ceremony accompanied the inaugural mission. American and Soviet generals and diplomats gathered at Poltava, exchanging congratulations, cigars, and bouquets of flowers.

Operation Frantic, however, was destined to fizzle after just four months. Only a handful of bombing and strafing missions were conducted by 10 B-17 bomber groups and their accompanying fighter support. Four days after the opening ceremonies, US bombers hit an enemy air base in Romania. They conducted another raid five days later, and on June 21, 1944, Flying Fortresses bombed the Nazi capital of Berlin. The raiders were unaware that they were shadowed by a German Heinkel He-177 long-range reconnaissance aircraft.

Once the Germans discovered the Soviet airfields, the Poltava and Mirgorod locations were photographed, and a destructive retaliatory Luftwaffe raid wreaked havoc. At Poltava 47 B-17s were destroyed on the ground. The Soviets and Americans bickered over the lack of security that had led to the debacle, and the last Operation Frantic raid occurred in September 1944. By then, Allied ground forces were advancing swiftly, overrunning many of its intended targets and erasing the raison d'etre for the initiative.

U-505 CAPTURED ON HIGH SEAS

When Task Group 22.3 captured the submarine U-505 on the high seas west of Cape Blanco off the coast of French West Africa, it was the first such seizure of an enemy naval vessel by the US Navy since the War of 1812.

By 1944, the Allies had gained the upper hand in the Battle of the Atlantic, turning the tables on the U-boats of the Nazi Kriegsmarine that for many months had ravaged merchant shipping convoys in transit across the sea. New weapons in the war against the marauding U-boats as well as improved tactics had given Allied naval hunter-killer groups the edge. Task Group 22.3, under the command of Captain Daniel V. Gallery, had been organised in late 1943 and put to sea for the first time the following January. A formidable naval force dedicated to the fight against the U-boats, Task Group 22.3 included the new escort aircraft carrier USS *Guadalcanal* and the swift destroyer escorts *Chatelain*, *Pillsbury*, *Flaherty*, *Pope*, and *Jenks*, each capable of speeds up to 25kts.

Above: A US Navy boarding party works aboard the recently captured U-505 in the Atlantic. (Public Domain US Navy via Wikimedia Commons)

Left: Captain Daniel Gallery stands in the conning tower of the captured U-505. (Public Domain US Navy via Wikimedia Commons)

Running low on fuel on the morning of June 4, 1944, Task Group 22.3 was tracking a sonar contact. Gallery was reluctant to turn toward port at Casablanca, and at 11:10 a flash was received from *Chatelain*. The U-boat contact had been fixed, and Chatelain wheeled to launch a pattern of 20 hedgehog bomblets at the target. Grumman F4F Wildcat fighters from *Guadalcanal* marked the location with bursts of machine-gun fire, and two more destroyer escorts joined in the chase. *Chatelain* turned again as sailors rolled a dozen depth charges off the stern.

Seconds later, the detonations inflicted serious damage on the Type IXC submarine, blasting a hole in the outer hull. The U-505 commander, Lieutenant Harald Lange, had no choice but to surface. Just 11 minutes after the first attack, the U-boat bobbed up, stern first. Hatches flew open, and crewmen spilled onto the deck. Lange was wounded by machine-gun fire and dragged into the water by two crewmen.

Captain Gallery had ordered the destroyer escort crews to train boarding parties, and it appeared that they now had their chance. Although U-505 was taking on water, the stricken submarine might still be boarded and captured. While Flaherty stayed with *Guadalcanal* and Pope took up station two miles distant to maintain watch for other U-boats, the crews of *Chatelain*, *Pillsbury*, and *Jenks* mustered their boarding parties and made ready their whaleboats. As German sailors stood on deck with their hands raised, Gallery ordered his ships to cease fire and shouted: "Away boarders!"

The first boarding party to reach U-505 was led by Lieutenant (j.g.) Albert David from Pillsbury. A sailor jumped aboard the submarine

The German submarine U-*505* is brought alongside the escort carrier USS Guadalcanal on June 4, 1944. (Public Domain US Navy via Wikimedia Commons)

Captain Daniel Gallery and Lieutenant Albert David are shown on the bridge of USS *Guadalcanal*. (Public Domain US Navy via Wikimedia Commons)

and tied a length of rope to the U-boat's stern. Gallery whooped: "Hi-ho Silver! Ride 'em Cowboy!"

Weapons drawn, the rest of the boarding party scrambled aboard the U-boat, disregarding the possibility of booby traps or more Germans below deck. They descended through the conning tower and into the control room, closed the sea cocks that the enemy crew had opened in an effort to scuttle the submarine, and then gathered code books, Enigma encoding machines, charts, and other intelligence. They also unjammed the submarine's rudder, easing the towing process. Twenty more American sailors soon reached the submarine, and David later received the Medal of Honor for gallantry.

While *Chatelain*, *Pillsbury*, and *Jenks* picked up German prisoners, *Pillsbury* tried to get a tow line in place, but the U-*505*'s bow planes sliced into the little warship's hull, flooding two main compartments. As the destroyer escort backed away, *Guadalcanal* approached. A steel cable was threaded through the submarine's bullnose, and the tow was secured as the US flag was run up from its bridge.

The fuel situation remained serious, and Casablanca was too distant. Gallery radioed Atlantic Fleet headquarters for permission to put in at Dakar, Senegal, on the West African coast. The request was denied since Dakar was rife with Nazi spies who might alert Berlin that the Enigma equipment and codes had been compromised, although the Allies had already been deciphering German radio traffic for some time. Instead, Gallery was instructed to rendezvous with a tanker at sea and then proceed to Bermuda, 2,500 miles away. On June 19, *Guadalcanal* and the destroyer escorts of Task Group 22.3 steamed into safe harbour. The task group later received the Presidential Unit Citation, while Gallery was awarded the Distinguished Service Medal.

The Allies kept the capture of the U-*505* quiet for the duration of the war. In fact, Gallery narrowly averted a court martial after

The U-*505* sits on display today at the Museum of Science and Technology in Chicago. (Creative Commons Jeremy Atherton via Wikimedia Commons)

he received a tongue lashing from Admiral Ernest J. King, Chief of Naval Operations, for putting the Enigma intelligence coup at risk. Nevertheless, Gallery went on to command the Essex-class aircraft carrier USS *Hancock* in the Pacific and was promoted rear admiral in December 1945.

After the war, Gallery and Lange met in Germany, dined and attended a theatre production together, and became good friends. U-*505* spent a decade in neglect at the Portsmouth Navy Yard in Maine. The submarine was later moved to Chicago, Gallery's hometown, and placed on permanent display at the Museum of Science and Industry.

The destroyer escort USS *Chatelain* participated in the capture of U-*505* on the high seas. (Public Domain US Navy via Wikimedia Commons)

THE LIBERATION OF ROME

In the evening of June 4, 1944, elements of the First Special Service Force, 3rd Infantry Division, and 88th Division of the US II Corps, Fifth Army entered Rome at multiple points in as sporadic German resistance was brushed aside. The VI Corps were not far behind. By 11pm, all bridges across the River Tiber in both corps operations areas had been secured.

General Fred Walker, commander of the 36th Division, remembered his own entry into the Eternal City: "As we moved along the dark streets, we could hear the people at all the windows of the high buildings clapping their hands." Finally, after nine months of arduous, bloody fighting, five American divisions of the Fifth Army and the US-Canadian 1st Special Service Force had taken the one-time capital of Mussolini's fascist Italy.

Just a day earlier, when it had become apparent that Rome would be lost, Field Marshal Albert Kesselring, commander of German forces in the Mediterranean, had declared Rome an open city. Even Adolf Hitler in far-off Berlin recognised the cultural significance of the Eternal City and issued orders to safeguard its treasures. Both the Allies and the Germans made assurances to the Vatican that its sanctity would be respected.

Meanwhile, the citizens of Rome spilled into the streets, celebrating, dancing, and embracing friends and strangers alike. Emerging from their shuttered homes, they brought food and wine to the Allied soldiers in an atmosphere of joy.

General Mark Clark, commander of Fifth Army, rolled into Rome in a Jeep on the afternoon of June 4, pausing for a photo opportunity. The next day, he called his corps commanders and staff officers together at city hall atop the Capitoline Hill. From the vantage point, the liberators watched the continuing celebration, but to a man they knew that the moment of glory was fleeting. Operation Overlord, the invasion of Normandy, was only hours away, and by June 6, 1944, the Italian campaign would fade from the newspaper headlines and become a sideshow.

By the afternoon of June 5, columns of Allied soldiers and vehicles were streaming through the streets of Rome, some of them skirting the ancient Colosseum. They were in pursuit of the regrouping Germans who had established a line of resistance along a 20-mile front from the mouth of the Tiber in the southwest to its confluence with the River Aniene in the northeast.

Obsessed with Rome from the beginning, General Clark had achieved his great victory and the momentary prestige that accompanied it. However, his decision to divert from the original plan of Operation Buffalo, the breakout from the Anzio beachhead,

General Mark Clark, commander of the Allied Fifth Army, arrives in Rome on the afternoon of June 4, 1944. (Public Domain US Army via Wikimedia Commons)

Above: Field Marshal Albert Kesselring confers with General Heinrich von Vietinghoff, commander of the German Tenth Army, in Italy. (Public Domain National Digital Archives of Poland via Wikimedia Commons)

Left: American tank destroyers roll past the ancient Colosseum on the day after Rome's liberation in 1944. (Public Domain US Army via Wikimedia Commons)

had generated significant controversy. Clark had always doubted the opinion of his superior officer, General Sir Harold Alexander, commanding 15th Army Group, that a concerted drive on the town of Valmontone, northwest of Anzio, and control of Highway 6 would trap thousands of German troops in southern Italy.

Operation Buffalo had gotten underway on May 23, complementing Operation Diadem, Alexander's direct broad assault on the Gustav Line by Fifth and Eighth Armies south of Rome. The linkup of the VI Corps from Anzio and Fifth Army was accomplished two days later, but Clark was already chafing to change the VI Corps axis of advance to the northwest and Rome, diverting the bulk of his forces from the advance on Valmontone.

Late on the afternoon of May 24, Clark ordered General Lucian Truscott, commanding VI Corps, to shift his advance toward Rome along with the balance of Fifth Army, including the 34th, 36th, 45th, 85th, and 88th Infantry Divisions and 1st Armored Division. The 3rd Infantry Division and First Special Service Force would continue to Valmontone.

The *Official History of the US Army in World War Two* later noted: "Truscott was dumbfounded…this was no time, the corps commander argued, to shift the main effort of his attack to the northwest…where

Above: A British soldier inspects the wreckage of a German 88mm gun abandoned during the retreat from Rome. (Public Domain collections of the Imperial War Museums via Wikimedia Commons)

Left: Days before their evacuation of Rome, German soldiers sit atop a tank adjacent to the Colosseum. (Creative Commons Bundesarchiv Bild via Wikimedia Commons)

persuaded Alexander to give Fifth Army exclusive use of Highway 6, the key roadway into Rome. From that time, the three corps of Fifth Army were reoriented and advancing on Rome via both highways 6 and 7.

As the German Fourteenth Army fell back through the Alban Hills and across the Tiber, Tenth Army broke contact with the Eighth Army forces on its front an also began to retire in orderly fashion. By dawn on June 3, II and VI Corps had begun their final race for Rome. Soon enough, the Eternal City was in Allied hands.

the enemy was still strong. The offensive should continue instead with 'maximum power' into the Valmontone Gap to insure the destruction of the German Army."

However, like the good soldier he was, Truscott obeyed. Alexander realised there was nothing he could do to stop Clark. At the same time, other high-level Allied officers, and even British Prime Minister Winston Churchill, were shocked by Clark's decision. One observer remarked that the vainglorious general: "overnight threw away the chance of destroying the right wing of [German General Heinrich] von Vietinghoff's Tenth Army for the honour of entering Rome first."

In the event, stubborn German resistance did slow the approach to Rome as the defenders occupied positions before the Alban Hills along the Caesar Line, still under construction in some places, and elsewhere. When a gap in the line was discovered, American troops were already through it before the Germans could slam the door. At the end of May, Clark

After the liberation of Rome, two American soldiers converse with a British soldier in St Peter's Square, Vatican City. (Public Domain collections of the Imperial War Museums via Wikimedia Commons)

OPERATION OVERLORD: D-DAY

In the early hours of June 6, 1944, and following an extended air and naval bombardment, Allied troops came ashore along a 50-mile stretch of the coastline of French Normandy. After months of planning and logistical buildup of men and materiel in Britain, Operation Overlord, the assault on Hitler's 'Fortress Europe', was unleashed. General Dwight D. Eisenhower, Supreme Commander of Allied Forces in Europe, had ordered the airborne and amphibious operations of D-Day forward amid weather conditions that were far from ideal.

Following a 24-hour postponement due to the worst June weather in the English Channel in half a century, 150,000 Allied soldiers hit the beaches, designated Sword, Juno, Gold, Omaha, and Utah. In the predawn hours, the Allied vanguard, three airborne divisions, had parachuted into Normandy behind the beach defences to seize key locations to facilitate the inland movement of the troops coming ashore.

Left: General Dwight Eisenhower visits paratroopers of the US 101st Airborne Division prior to D-Day. (Public Domain US Army via Wikimedia Commons)

Below: Allied Sherman DD tanks are loaded aboard transports for the cross-Channel invasion of June 6, 1944. (Public Domain US Army Signal Corps via Wikimedia Commons)

Soldiers of the US 1st Infantry Division wade ashore at Omaha Beach on June 6, 1944. (Public Domain US Coast Guard via Wikimedia Commons)

The invasion was fraught with risk, and the weather conditions complicated matters significantly. At 4:15am on June 5, Eisenhower had assembled his most senior lieutenants for their seventh meeting in the runup to the invasion. He asked them individually to express opinions on moving forward with the invasion during a window of favourable weather on June 6. Combat troops were already aboard ships, and the next suitable tides and atmospheric conditions were two weeks away. Eisenhower weighed the situation and pronounced: "Okay, we'll go!"

Omaha Beach is crowded with men and equipment after the D-Day landings have secured a lodgement in Normandy. (Public Domain US Coast Guard via Wikimedia Commons)

At the same time, Eisenhower was aware of the real prospect of defeat and accepted full responsibility for the outcome. He scribbled a note for release to the media in the event of a major setback. It read: "Our landings in the Cherbourg-Havre area have failed to gain a satisfactory foothold and I have withdrawn the troops. My decision to attack at this time and place was based upon the best information available. The troops, the air and the navy did all that bravery and devotion to duty could do. If any blame or fault attaches to the attempt it is mine alone."

The landings were hotly contested, but the statement was never publicly read. Eisenhower later gave it to a subordinate as a memento.

Operation Overlord commenced at approximately 11pm on June 5 as Allied planes took off from their airfields across Britain loaded with 20,000 paratroopers of the British 6th and American 82nd and 101st Airborne Divisions. The 6th Airborne was assigned to seize bridges across the River Orne, the Orne Canal, and other waterways while controlling high ground between the Orne and the River Dives to secure the left flank of the invasion. The 101st was to take key causeways, or exits, from

Above: Paras of the British 6th Airborne Division receive a briefing prior to D-Day. (Public Domain collections of the Imperial War Museums via Wikimedia Commons)

Left: Soldiers of the US 4th Infantry Division climb over the sea wall at Utah Beach and move inland. (Public Domain US Army Signal Corps via Wikimedia Commons)

Utah beach, facilitating the advance of the US 4th Infantry Division, while the 82nd was tasked with the capture of the French village of Ste Mere-Église and key bridges across the River Merderet. These movements would secure the right flank of the invasion.

The transport planes and gliders were buffeted by high winds and German anti-aircraft fire. The airborne troops were scattered across a wide swathe of Normandy. However, bands of troopers, some combining elements of different units, moved out under capable officers to seize their objectives. In a remarkable feat of airmanship at the Benouville Bridge across the Caen Canal and the bridge over the Orne, Sergeant Jim Wallwork brought his glider down just 50 yards from the canal bridge. Other glider pilots executed pinpoint landings as well.

After surrendering to Canadian forces in Normandy, German prisoners are marched to the rear. (Public Domain Library and Archives of Canada via Wikimedia Commons)

Royal Marine Commandos move inland from Sword Beach in Normandy on the morning of June 6, 1944. (Public Domain collections of the Imperial War Museums via Wikimedia Commons)

Lieutenant Dan Brotheridge led 30 men of the 1st Platoon, 2nd Oxfordshire and Buckinghamshire Light Infantry in a rush to take the span. Brotheridge was shot in the neck and became the first Allied soldier to die on D-Day. Both bridges were taken. Meanwhile, Lieutenant Colonel Terence Otway led the 9th Battalion, 3rd Brigade, Parachute Regiment, in silencing the Merville Battery, a fortified German emplacement whose guns threatened the invasion beaches.

The 82nd Airborne seized Ste Mere-Église and held out against vicious German counterattacks while also gaining a toehold across the Dives at Chef-du-Pont after eight hours of fighting. The 101st captured causeways and linked up with the 4th Division. Lieutenant Colonel Robert Cole, commanding the 502nd Parachute Infantry Regiment, led an ad hoc group of troopers from both US airborne divisions and met the advancing infantrymen at about 1pm on D-Day.

More than 7,000 Allied ships had assembled off the coast of Normandy, and the first Allied troops to come ashore, soldiers of the 8th Infantry Regiment, 4th Division under the command of Colonel James Van Fleet, touched French soil at 6:30am. Strong currents pushed the first 20 landing craft 2,000 yards east of the intended Utah Beach landing zone, but Van Fleet and General Theodore Roosevelt, Jr., assistant commander of the 4th Division, decided to "start the war from here" rather than redirecting subsequent waves to the original location.

Although elements of the German 91st Airlanding, 243rd, and 709th Divisions defended Utah Beach, the misdirection aided the

Americans, and resistance was light. The 4th Division was responsible for transiting the causeways off Utah Beach and securing coastal roads near Ste Mere-Église and Carentan and preparing for a concentrated attack on the major port of Cherbourg. By late morning, three of the four causeways were in American hands, and the linkup with elements of the 101st Airborne was effected near the town of Pouppeville.

The costliest fighting of D-Day occurred at Omaha Beach, east of Utah. The German 352nd Infantry Division occupied strong fortifications, and the Americans of the 1st and 29th Infantry Divisions were raked with machine-gun, rifle, mortar and cannon rounds from positions with interlocking fields of fire. The first wave foundered, and casualties were heavy as infantrymen struggled through the surf and sought cover among the steel landing obstacles that dotted the shore. Some landing craft were riddled well out from the beach; others drifted off course. Some stopped short of the beach and disgorged their infantrymen, with full packs, into water well above their heads – many drowning under the weight.

Compounding the issues at Omaha, only two of the 29 amphibious DD (duplex-drive) Sherman tanks of the 741st Tank Battalion, intended to support the infantrymen on the beach, managed to reach shore. The others were swamped in the choppy surf and sank to the bottom of the English Channel. In contrast, 27 DD Shermans of the 743rd Tank Battalion made it ashore at Utah Beach.

In Dog sector of Omaha Beach, the 116th Infantry Regiment, 29th Division, hit the surf under withering fire. One landing craft took a direct hit and simply disintegrated. Another was sunk with all 32 men aboard, including a company commander. Company A, 116th Infantry, came ashore at Dog Green Beach and lost 65% of its strength in 10 harrowing minutes. Twenty-two of its dead were from the tiny town of Bedford, Virginia, population only 3,200. The story of the 'Bedford Boys' became symbolic of the sacrifice of so many during the 'Longest Day'.

For more than an hour there was no appreciable movement off Omaha Beach.

General Omar Bradley, commanding American ground troops on D-Day, watched from the cruiser Augusta. He contemplated evacuating the soldiers from Omaha and diverting subsequent waves elsewhere. However, at around 8am, General Norman Cota, assistant commander of the 29th Division, rallied the advance off Dog Green, while junior and non-commissioned officers displayed initiative elsewhere, spurring groups of soldiers to move forward and silence enemy guns. By the end of the day, 2,500 Americans had been killed, wounded, or missing, but a small beachhead 1,500 by 2,000 yards had been established.

In the centre of the D-Day landing beaches, the five-mile length of Gold Beach was assaulted by the British 50th Division, including the East Yorkshire, Devonshire, Dorsetshire, and Hampshire Regiments with No. 47 Royal Marine Commando. Early objectives included cutting the road between the cities of Caen and Bayeux, capturing the

A tank comes ashore at Gold Beach after British troops have secured the area on D-Day. (Public Domain collections of the Imperial War Museums via Wikimedia Commons)

US paratroopers meet members of the French resistance in Normandy during Operation Overlord. (Public Domain US Army Signal Corps via Wikimedia Commons)

coastal town of Arromanches, destroying a battery of German guns at Longues-sur-Mer, and linking up with the Americans at Omaha Beach to the west and the Canadians at Juno Beach to the east.

At Gold Beach, the effectiveness of pre-invasion naval bombardment was remarkable, the light cruiser HMS *Ajax* putting six-inch shells directly through two of the four casemates of the Longues-sur-Mer battery. The Commandos took high ground at Port-en-Bessin and joined with the Canadians at Juno Beach. By nightfall, the penetration was six miles inland. The road between Caen and Bayeux had not been reached, nor had a junction with the Americans at Omaha Beach occurred, but the assault on Gold Beach had achieved excellent results.

East of Gold Beach, the Canadian 3rd Infantry Division attacked a six-mile stretch of Juno Beach from Saint-Aubin in the east to La Riviere in the west. Aside from the Americans at Omaha, the Canadians at Juno experienced the fiercest German resistance of D-Day. The North Shore Regiment, Queen's Own Rifles, Regina Rifles, and Royal Winnipeg Rifles landed in two sectors, Nan and Mike, while companies of the Canadian Scottish Regiment and No. 48 Royal Marine Commando held the flanks. The German defenders of the 716th Division wreaked havoc for two hours from fortified bunkers, machine-gun nests, and positions in beachfront houses. Company B, Royal Winnipeg Rifles, was reduced to a single officer and 25 soldiers in its dash for the protection of a low sea wall.

At the end of the day, the Canadians had advanced inland more than nine miles from Juno Beach, the deepest penetration of the day. Contact with the 50th Division was established, but the objective of the Carpiquet airfield was still in German hands, and a dangerous three-mile gap existed between the Canadians at Juno and British troops at Sword Beach. The Canadians suffered 1,200 casualties.

The first troops of the British 3rd Division hit Sword, the easternmost of the invasion beaches, at 7:25am, and within 45 minutes they were

pushing inland with the support of the 27th Armoured Brigade, tasked with capturing Caen and converging on Carpiquet airfield to meet the Canadians from Juno. Meanwhile, the 1st Special Service Brigade, including Commando units under Simon Fraser, Lord Lovat, had been assigned the relief of the 6th Airborne Paras holding the bridges over the Caen Canal and the Orne. This was accomplished about 1:30pm.

By afternoon, the Stafford Yeomanry and the King's Shropshire Light Infantry had advanced toward Caen and Carpiquet but were stopped short of the linkup with the Canadians. The advance had run into the only German armoured counterattack of D-Day as elements of the 21st Panzer Division moved forward, actually reaching the coast between Sword and Juno beaches near nightfall. However, no reinforcements were available to exploit the gain, and the Germans were forced to withdraw. The British had suffered only 630 casualties at Sword. However, weeks of fighting would be required before Caen – a D-Day objective – belonged to the Allies.

Operation Overlord and the Normandy campaign were underway with the successful D-Day landings, and Allied casualties had been surprisingly light with only 4,900 killed, wounded, or captured.

Contributing to the achievement, Eisenhower and his subordinates had boldly accepted the risks associated with the landings in conditions that were less than ideal, while the Germans had been taken by surprise. An elaborate deception, Operation Fortitude, had convinced many high-ranking German officers, and Hitler himself, that the main Allied landings would occur to the north at the Pas-de-Calais. Hitler had retained personal control of nearly all the German armoured forces, refusing to release them in response to the Normandy landings until it was too late to potentially drive the Allies into the sea.

During the coming weeks, Allied forces slugged their way through the hedgerow country, or bocage, of Normandy, fighting pitched battles for control of Caen, Carentan, and other important objectives before breaking out of the lodgement in late July.

Above: General Eisenhower and senior Allied commanders sent Allied forces into action on D-Day in Normandy. (Public Domain collections of the Imperial War Museums via Wikimedia Commons)

Below: Troops of the 9th Canadian Infantry Brigade wade ashore at Juno Beach in Normandy on June 6, 1944. (Public Domain Government of the United Kingdom via Wikimedia Commons)

ORADOUR-SUR-GLANE MASSACRE

In the wake of the D-Day invasion, French resistance groups stepped up their activities, derailing locomotives, cutting communications lines, and ambushing German soldiers wherever possible. Delayed continually by such acts along with destructive Allied air attacks, the 2nd SS Panzer Division Das Reich, en route to reinforce German defences in Normandy, halted at the small French village of Oradour-sur-Glane to execute a brutal reprisal for the apparent kidnapping of a German officer.

Oradour-sur-Glane, a tiny settlement in west-central France, lies along the route of the Das Reich trek toward Normandy from Toulouse in the south of France, and on this fateful morning its 4th SS Panzergrenadier Regiment Der Fuhrer, under the command of Major Adolf Diekmann, rumbled into the heart of the village, intent on teaching the French a terrible lesson.

The ruins of Oradour-sur-Glane remain as a memorial to those murdered in 1944. (Public Domain Dennis Nilsson via Wikimedia Commons)

In one of the most heinous atrocities of World War Two, Dickmann ordered the murders of 642 men, women, and children, virtually wiping out the local population. The men were herded at gunpoint into several barns and outbuildings, cut down by machine-gun fire, and their bodies set ablaze. The women and children were locked inside the local church, which was put to the torch, and burned alive. Those who managed to escape momentarily were shot dead as they ran into the open. Only one woman survived the massacre.

By June 11 (D+5), as the Allies worked feverishly to consolidate their beachhead in French Normandy, 326,000 combat troops were ashore along with 100,000 tons of supplies and equipment and 50,000 vehicles. On June 13, the town of Carentan fell after four days of bitter fighting, and the convergence of the Allied V and VII Corps stretched the lodgement on the European continent to an unbroken length of 60 miles with a penetration of 10 miles at its shallowest point.

Das Reich was ordered to move to Normandy as rapidly as possible, but its progress was slowed from the outset as the Germans were set upon by Allied air power, which prevented the division's tanks from being loaded on rail cars for at least 10 days. While German troops or vehicles caught in the open during daylight hours were bombed and strafed relentlessly, the French resistance had continually harassed Das Reich troop movements as well.

The massacre at Oradour-sur-Glane was one of numerous SS war crimes committed during the Normandy campaign. Diekmann was killed in action a few days later, but after the war, 65 of the 200 surviving SS men that participated in the atrocity were arrested and tried. Twenty were found guilty of war crimes and sentenced to prison, the last of them released in 1958. Through the years, two more trials were conducted. One resulted in a life sentence, but the charges were dropped in the other.

Oradour-sur-Glane was never rebuilt, and its stark ruins remain today as a memorial.

Above: Major Adolf Diekmann led the SS troops that slaughtered the citizens of Oradour-sur-Glane. (Public Domain Jdh009 Unknown Author via Wikimedia Commons)

Left: Burned during the 1944 massacre, the hulk of a car rusts on the street in Oradour-sur-Glane. (Creative Commons TwoWings via Wikimedia Commons)

US FORCES LAND ON SAIPAN IN THE MARIANAS

On this day, the US 2nd and 4th Marine Divisions, V Amphibious Corps landed on the beaches of Saipan in the Mariana Islands of the Central Pacific. Only 1,200 miles from the Japanese home islands. The seizure of Saipan and nearby Guam and Tinian, along with their airfields, would bring the cities of Japan and the nation's military-industrial complex within range of the big Boeing B-29 Superfortress bombers destined to rain destruction on the enemy in the remaining months of World War Two.

The Marines were led by General Holland M. 'Howlin' Mad' Smith, commander of the V Amphibious Corps, while General Thomas Watson led the 2nd Division and General Harry Schmidt commanded the 4th Division. The US Army's 27th Infantry Division, under the command of General Ralph Smith, was initially held in reserve but committed early in the fight as the Americans confronted nearly 23,000 Japanese troops of the 31st Army under General Hideyoshi Obata. The invasion occurred while Obata was absent on an inspection tour, and tactical command devolved to General Yoshitsugu Saito.

The landings were hotly contested, but the Marines pushed inland, capturing the village of Charon Kanoa and destroying some enemy

bunkers and machine-gun nests. At times the fighting was close-quarter, and a few Marines armed with shotguns used them to good effect. Losses were heavy as the 6th Marine Regiment alone suffers 35% casualties, and the beachhead encompassed only about half the anticipated gains by the end of the first day.

General Holland Smith committed the bulk of the 27th Division to the fight on June 16, and during the night the Japanese mounted a major counterattack. General Saito assembled the 44 light and medium tanks of the 9th Tank Regiment along with the troops of the 1st Yokosuka

Right: US Marines and their equipment are shown on the beach at Saipan on June 15, 1944. (Public Domain US Department of Defense via Wikimedia Commons)

Below: This oil painting depicts the arrival of supplies and troops at Saipan in the Marianas. (Public Domain William F. Draper Naval History and Heritage Command via Wikimedia Commons)

US Marines take cover behind a Sherman tank during the fighting on Saipan. (Public Domain US Marine Corps National Archives and Records Administration via Wikimedia Commons)

Soldiers of the US Army's 27th Infantry Division advance along a dirt road on Saipan. (Public Domain US Department of Defense via Wikimedia Commons)

Special Naval Landing Force and elements of the 136th Division and unleashed them on the forward positions of the 4th Marine Division.

In the ensuing melee, a platoon of M4 Sherman tanks, mounting 75mm guns that were significantly heavier than anything the Japanese armoured vehicles carried, came to the support of the 1st Battalion, 6th Marines. Within minutes, 24 Japanese tanks were blazing hulks, and the accompanying infantry was shredded by small-arms, mortar, and artillery fire. The Marines lost 100 killed and wounded, but 60% of the attacking Japanese, roughly 300 men, were casualties.

Three weeks of hard fighting remained as the Americans slugged their way across the island and then pivoted north in the direction of the Japanese main line of defence. While the decisive Battle of the Philippine Sea raged offshore, the going was tough amid the rugged terrain of Saipan. The Marine divisions moved forward on each flank, but the progress of the Army's 27th Division in the centre was somewhat sluggish. Holland Smith blamed the perceived ineptitude of Ralph Smith and relieved the Army general of his duties, sparking a firestorm of interservice controversy that led to several formal inquiries. The debate as to whether Ralph Smith deserved to be sacked continues today; he was replaced by General Sanderford Jarman and later General George Griner.

The Americans fought stubborn Japanese resistance at locations that received highly descriptive nicknames, including Hell's Pocket, Purple Heart Ridge, and Death Valley. Grudgingly giving ground, the enemy yielded the Kagaman Peninsula to the 4th Marine Division on June 25; however, the Americans were still obliged to root the defenders out of remaining strongpoints with flamethrowers, satchel charges, and hand grenades. The Japanese had fortified the mouths of caves, and these were often sealed shut with high explosives.

By the end of June, the 2nd Marine Division was approaching the village of Garapan and engaged in a heated battle for nearby high ground dubbed Flame Tree Hill. The 105th Infantry Regiment, 27th Division had taken Nafutan Point and closed up with the 8th Marines to finish off the Japanese at Purple Heart Ridge and Death Valley, taking control of central Saipan. The 4th Division also advanced past the village of Tanapag in the west and then went into temporary reserve as preparations were made for the final push.

General Saito knew that the end was near and ordered his command to prepare a massive banzai charge against the American line. On the morning of July 6, he told his officers: "Whether we attack or whether we stay where we are, there is only death." A short time later, the general and other high-ranking officers committed ritual suicide, or seppuku.

The banzai attack went forward before dawn on July 7, the human tidal wave slashing into the American positions. Hundreds of Japanese soldiers, many of them fortified with sake (Japanese rice wine), screamed and ran forward only to be cut down by intense machine-gun and rifle fire. Still, the attackers broke through in some places, fighting hand-to-hand with Marine artillerymen behind the front line. By afternoon, it was over and more than 4,000 Japanese troops had been killed.

On the afternoon of July 9, Saipan was declared secure. However, the Americans had witnessed a grim spectacle. Hundreds of Japanese soldiers and civilian inhabitants of the island had committed suicide, hurling themselves from the high cliffs at Marpi Point or simply walking into the sea with babies in their arms. The Japanese had convinced the natives that the Americans would torture and murder them. Instead, those who remained were given food and medical attention.

It was a poignant coda to the costly fight and on Saipan, where US casualties totalled 3,225 dead and 13,061 wounded, the Japanese garrison was virtually annihilated.

US Marines survey the mouth of a cave that once concealed Japanese defenders on Saipan. (Public Domain US Naval History and Heritage Command via Wikimedia Commons)

A Marine lieutenant aids a woman and her children during operations on Saipan. (Public Domain National Archives and Records Administration via Wikimedia Commons)

BATTLE OF THE PHILIPPINE SEA BEGINS

While the Marines and US Army troops of the V Amphibious Corps fought for control of Saipan, the US Navy's Fifth Fleet, commanded by Admiral Raymond A. Spruance, undertook dual missions, first to protect the supply ships and troop transports off the Marianas from Japanese attack, and second to engage and defeat the Imperial Japanese Navy should its forces attempt to intervene. Admiral Spruance fully expected the enemy to sortie, and four days after the Saipan landings, the Battle of the Philippine Sea, one of the great naval conflicts of World War Two, was underway.

After recovering from the disaster of Pearl Harbor and fighting their way across the Pacific for 30 months, the Americans had won victories in the Gilbert and Marshall Islands. Now possession of three key islands in the Marianas - Saipan, Guam, and Tinian - would provide airfields for long-range Boeing B-29 Superfortress bombers to carry the war to the home islands of Japan. Further, Japanese supply lines would

US Navy Lieutenant Alexander Vraciu signals that he has shot down six Japanese planes on June 19, 1944. (Public Domain US Navy via Wikimedia Commons)

Left: Admiral Raymond A. Spruance commanded the US Fifth Fleet at the Battle of the Philippine Sea. (Public Domain US Navy via Wikimedia Commons)

Below: Contrails cross the sky above the US Fifth Fleet as American and Japanese pilots duel during the Battle of the Philippine Sea. (Public Domain US Navy via Wikimedia Commons)

be threatened, and in conjunction with the seizure of the Palaus to the west, the flank of General Douglas MacArthur's southern thrust into the Philippines would be protected.

For months the Japanese had expected an offensive into the Marianas, and Admiral Soemu Toyoda, commander-in-chief of the Japanese Combined Fleet, set in motion Operation A-Go, a desperate bid to inflict a decisive naval defeat on the Americans and disrupt the Marianas operation. By mid-June, Admiral Jisaburo Ozawa, commander of the First Mobile Fleet, mustered a formidable armada including five fleet aircraft carriers, four light carriers, five battleships, 11 heavy cruisers, two light cruisers, and 28 destroyers, and weighed anchor for the Philippine Sea to confront the Fifth Fleet. The Japanese force also included the super battleships *Yamato* and *Musashi*, displacing 70,000 tons each, the largest warships of their kind ever built. On the decks of Ozawa's carriers were 500 combat aircraft, and he intended to draw on the strength of land-based planes in the Philippines and surrounding islands to attack the American fleet, utilising the advantage of the greater range possessed by the Japanese aircraft types.

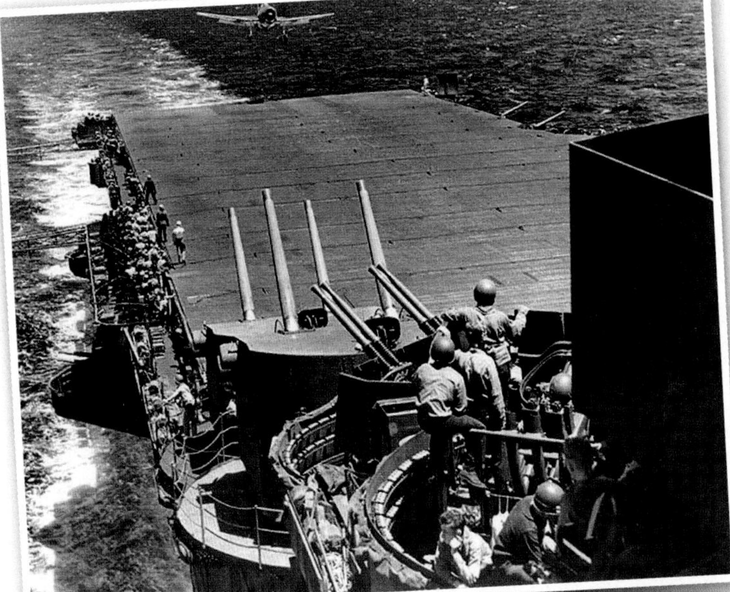

A Grumman F6F Hellcat fighter lands aboard the aircraft carrier USS *Lexington* during the Battle of the Philippine Sea. (Public Domain US Navy via Wikimedia Commons)

Aware of his primary mission, Spruance maintained a defensive posture. His Fifth Fleet, built around Task Force 58 and its four battle groups under the command of Admiral Marc Mitscher, included seven large fleet carriers, eight light carriers, seven battleships, 21 heavy and light cruisers, 69 destroyers, and nearly 1,000 aircraft, many of their types outclassing the Japanese opposition in firepower, durability, and overall performance. The superb Grumman F6F Hellcat fighter, for example, had made its combat debut just in August 1943.

US picket submarines and intelligence dispatches provided Spruance with ample warning of the Japanese approach, and on the morning of June 19, Ozawa launched 69 aircraft to attack the Fifth Fleet. American fighters were waiting and shot down 45 enemy planes in just a few minutes. A second Japanese strike of 127 planes also came to grief, most of its aircraft splashed under the guns of American fighters.

The Japanese mounted four major air raids on the American fleet during the Battle of the Philippine Sea and managed only to slightly damage a single carrier and two battleships. The aerial combat of June 19 was so one-sided that the US pilots dubbed the day's action the 'Great Marianas Turkey Shoot'. In retrospect, Ozawa's mission seemed doomed from the start. At this stage of the Pacific war most veteran Japanese pilots had been lost in earlier battles. Hastily trained newcomers were no match for the experienced US Navy airmen.

The Battle of the Philippine Sea broke the back of Japanese naval air power for the remainder of the war, while serious losses were also inflicted on the land-based planes that participated.

Compounding Ozawa's woes on June 19, the newest aircraft carrier of the Imperial Japanese Navy and his own flagship, *Taiho*, was torpedoed by the submarine USS *Albacore*, although the damage did not appear to be fatal. However, a young damage control officer ordered the big ship's ventilation system on to clear fumes from ruptured fuel lines. Soon the flammable vapours had coursed the length of *Taiho*; the ship became a floating bomb. A catastrophic explosion sent the carrier to the bottom within an hour. Just after noon, the submarine USS *Cavalla* put three torpedoes into the aircraft carrier *Shokaku*. A few hours later, *Shokaku* was wracked by an internal explosion and also sank.

Although American scout planes had been searching for Ozawa's task force, it was late in the day when the Japanese were finally located. Despite the fact that any US aircraft would be flying at the limit of their range and returning to their carriers in fading light, Mitscher ordered 240 planes into the air. As the sun was setting, the American torpedo and dive bombers pounced on the hapless Japanese, seriously damaging the carrier *Zuikaku*, the last survivor of the 1941 attack on Pearl Harbor, putting bombs into the light carriers *Junyo* and *Ryuho*, and sinking the light carrier *Hiyo*. The raiders returned in darkness with many pilots forced to ditch as fuel tanks ran dry. Others landed on any carrier deck they could find.

Mitscher courageously risked enemy submarine attack by ordering his ships to turn on their lights to help guide the pilots home. Eighty-two planes were lost, but most of the airmen were pulled from the water by destroyers the next morning.

During the two disastrous days of the Battle of the Philippine Sea, the Imperial Japanese Navy lost three aircraft carriers and more than 400 carrier-based planes. Ozawa had only 35 serviceable aircraft left. More than 200 land-based Japanese planes were destroyed. The Americans lost 130 planes and relatively few casualties.

Although Spruance has been criticised for not pursuing Ozawa and finishing off the Japanese carrier force, his primary responsibility was to defend the transports and supply vessels off Saipan. This he did, while delivering a near-fatal blow to the enemy.

The Japanese aircraft carrier *Zuikaku* and escorting destroyers are shown under attack during the Battle of the Philippine Sea. (Public Domain Naval History and Heritage Command via Wikimedia Commons)

Japanese cruisers steam in circles attempting to avoid attacks by US Navy aircraft during the Battle of the Philippine Sea, June 20, 1944. (Public Domain US Navy via Wikimedia Commons)

RED ARMY LAUNCHES OPERATION BAGRATION

In concert with the D-Day landings in Normandy, the Soviet Red Army launched Operation Bagration, one of the largest and most successful ground offensives of World War Two. As fighting slowed during the rainy season, the Soviets had made progress against German Army Groups North and South. Meanwhile, Army Group Centre occupied a salient that appeared vulnerable to attack, particularly as Hitler has been distracted with the Western Allied landings in Normandy and transferred some combat divisions to France to counter the emerging threat.

Soviet histories of the Great Patriotic War characterised 1944 as the 'Year of 10 Victories' or the year of 'Stalin's 10 Blows', and Operation Bagration was envisioned to maintain the Red Army's momentum, targeting the Army Group Centre salient and intended to eject the enemy from Belarus and eastern Poland. In April, Stavka, the Soviet high command, had begun assembling a massive force of 166 divisions – approximately 1.2 million troops – along with 6,000 Red Air Force planes, 4,000 tanks and self-propelled guns, and an estimated 31,000 artillery pieces.

Stalin named the looming offensive in honour of General Pyotr Bagration, a hero of the Napoleonic Wars, and waited until the third anniversary of Operation Barbarossa, the German assault on the Soviet Union in 1941, to unleash the sledgehammer of retribution. Operation Bagration concentrated on seizing four tactically critical points that

Soviet Field Marshal Aleksandr Vasilevsky and General Ivan Chernyakhovsky interrogated captured German General Alfons Hitter at Vitebsk. (Public Domain Archives of Ukraine via Wikimedia Commons)

Soviet troops and expatriate Poles fighting with the Red Army stride down a street in Vilnius, capital of Lithuania. (Public Domain Archives of Poland via Wikimedia Commons)

Soviet soldiers march forward on the northern flank of the Operation Bagration offensive. (Public Domain Archives of Belarus via Wikimedia Commons)

A Red Army soldier climbs atop a destroyed German PzKpfw IV tank after fighting near Bobruysk. (Public Domain Archives of Belarus via Wikimedia Commons)

would smash the German salient. These included the towns of Vitebsk, Orsha, Mogilev, and Bobruysk. Four Soviet army groups, or fronts, were assigned these objectives.

In the north, the 1st Baltic Front would shield the Red Army flank against interference from Army Group North while advancing north of Vitebsk. The 3rd Belorussian Front, commanded by General Ivan Chernyakhovsky, would attack from the south and link up with the 1st Baltic Front to encircle Vitebsk while driving through Orsha toward Minsk, the Belorussian capital city. Simultaneously, the 2nd Belorussian Front, led by General Georgy Zakharov, would sweep through Mogilev and join in the liberation of Minsk.

Marshal Konstantin Rokossovsky was to lead the 1st Belorussian Front in an encirclement and reduction of German defences at Bobruysk and then head for Minsk as well. Rokossovsky, of Polish birth, maintained a somewhat unique relationship with Stalin. While most of the Soviet premier's military commanders cowered before the dictator, Rokossovsky dared to disagree at times. During the planning for Bagration, Rokossovsky argued for two major points of penetration against the German lines, openly contradicting Stalin's opinion. Rokossovsky got his way.

Directly opposing the Soviet offensive, Army Group Centre, under the command of General Ernst von Busch, mustered roughly 580,000 men, but only 214,000 of these were combat infantrymen. The Germans were also significantly outnumbered in armoured vehicles and artillery.

Abandoned vehicles and equipment lie in the wake of the retreating German Ninth Army near Bobruysk. (Public Domain Archives of Belarus via Wikimedia Commons)

Although intelligence reports had warned that a major enemy attack was looming, there was little Busch could do. His front stretched 650 miles, and his 38 infantry and two panzer divisions were inadequate to defend such an area. Hitler had disagreed with the intelligence assessments and ordered substantial forces south to defend the oil fields of Romania, where he believed the next great Soviet offensive would come.

At 5 am on June 22, the Soviet storm broke with a massive artillery barrage that devastated many frontline German positions. By the following day, Vitebsk was encircled. When the city fell on June 27, the Germans had suffered 20,000 killed and wounded while another 10,000 soldiers were taken prisoner.

Also on the 27th, the 3rd Belorussian Front took Orsha while the 2nd Belorussian Front crossed the River Dnieper and was poised to assault Mogilev. The going was a bit tougher for Rokossovsky, whose spearheads had run into the veteran German Ninth Army. However, by the 27th, the 1st Belorussian Front managed to reach a junction with the Sixty-Fifth Army, trapping 40,000 German soldiers in Bobruysk. The Red Army advanced 95 miles in the first five days of Operation Bagration, and Hitler sacked Busch, replacing him with Field Marshal Walter Model.

For the Germans, the situation continued to deteriorate. A gap 250 miles wide had been torn in their front. Mogilev fell to the Soviets on June 28, and the reduction of the Bobruysk pocket was completed the next day with only 6,000 German soldiers left to surrender. Soviet tanks raced toward Minsk, and the city was liberated on July 3. More than 100,000 Germans were killed or captured east of the River Berezina and at Minsk. In six weeks, the 1st Baltic Front reached Vilnius, the capital of Lithuania, and the Gulf of Riga.

In mid-July, Marshal Ivan Koniev's 1st Ukrainian Front began clearing western Ukraine of enemy troops. German formations were cut off and annihilated or thrown back to the River Bug, and the city of Lvov fell at the end of the month. By July 25, Koniev and Rokossovsky were on the banks of the Vistula, and their two army fronts forced crossings of the river about 110 miles from Warsaw. The spearheads were halted on Stalin's order short of the Polish capital to allow the city's armed uprising to be brutally suppressed by the Nazis.

As Army Group Centre pulled back, Soviet advances cut off Army Group North in Estonia, its force of 33 understrength divisions too weak to mount an offensive. Army Group North remained isolated until the end of the war.

Operation Bagration concluded in mid-August, while Red Army drives north and south of the main offensive had also yielded substantial gains. At the end of the month, the Romanian government switched to the Allied side. Bulgaria followed a month later, and an armistice with Finland was also signed in September.

Thousands of German prisoners captured during Operation Bagration are paraded through the streets of Moscow in July 1944. (Creative Commons RIA Novosti archive image 129359 Michael Trahman via Wikimedia Commons)

LIBERATION OF CHERBOURG

With the capture of the city's fortified arsenal, organised resistance of Cherbourg ended and the deep-water port on the northern coast of the Cotentin Peninsula belonged to the Allies. Expecting a more desperate fight, in keeping with recent combat in the city, the American soldiers of the 47th Infantry Regiment were surprised when the garrison displayed white flags and more than 400 German soldiers emerged with their hands up to surrender.

Hours earlier, the commander of the Germans defending Cherbourg Fortress, General Karl-Wilhelm von Schlieben, and Admiral Walter Hennecke, commander of the Kriegsmarine naval defences of the port of Cherbourg, along with 800 more enemy troops had capitulated just before the entrances to their underground shelter were to be blasted by TNT. Schlieben had refused an earlier surrender demand, but a few rounds from US tank destroyers were convincing enough of the futility of further resistance.

Cherbourg had been a major objective of the Allied landings in Normandy since intensive planning had been undertaken in 1942. Although the Norman coastline offered some advantages, the absence of a major port for offloading reinforcements and supplies for the Allied offensive drive across France to the frontier of Germany was problematic. A temporary solution had been determined with the installation of artificial Mulberry harbours off Omaha and Gold Beaches. However, a howling gale completely destroyed the harbour at Omaha and seriously damaged the one installed at Gold in mid-June.

Meanwhile, the early objectives for Operation Overlord had been ambitious to say the least. The US VII Corps, under General J. Lawton Collins, had been expected to capture the port in nine days after the 4th Infantry Division came ashore at Utah Beach on D-Day and three follow-on divisions were quickly deployed to strengthen the thrust across the Cotentin Peninsula that would isolate its northern portion, including Cherbourg, facilitating the final seizure of the port. After linking up with the 82nd Airborne Division and fighting its way across the Rivers Merderet and Douve, the vanguard of VII Corps reached the town of Barneville on the peninsula's west coast and then pivoted north toward Cherbourg.

Wary of German snipers, American soldiers advance through the city streets of Cherbourg. (Public Domain US Army Signal Corps via Wikimedia Commons)

Three US infantry divisions had surrounded the port city by June 22, and Allied bombs plastered the German blockhouses, pillboxes, and bunkers. German shore batteries duelled with the US battleships *Texas*, *Arkansas*, and *Nevada*, as well as cruisers of the Royal Navy. The Germans resisted stubbornly, but the noose around Cherbourg tightened as squads of infantrymen took out strongpoints with satchel charges or tanks blasted entrances and gun embrasures at point-blank range.

Although two weeks behind schedule, Cherbourg was finally in Allied hands. However, immediate use of the port had been thwarted. Admiral Hennecke had followed orders for the systematic destruction of all equipment, machinery, and facilities that might be of use. Colonel Alvin G. Viney who prepared the original plan for the reconstruction of the port, wrote later: "The demolition of the port is a masterful job, beyond a doubt the most complete, intensive, and best-planned demolition in history." Cherbourg was not in shape to receive Allied shipping for many days.

General J. Lawton Collins, commander of the US VII Corps, receives the surrender of Cherbourg from General Karl-Wilhelm von Schlieben and Admiral Walter Hennecke. (Public Domain US Government via Wikimedia Commons)

American and German officers discuss surrender logistics in Cherbourg. (Public Domain Archives Normandie 1939-45 via Wikimedia Commons)

CAEN CAPTURED

After weeks of bloody fighting and heavy casualties on both sides, the transportation and communications centre of Caen fell to the Allies on July 9, 1944. Seven miles from the coastline of France and directly in the path of the 21st Army Group coming ashore at Gold, Juno, and Sword Beaches, Caen had been a D-Day objective. Tactically, the city was only 120 road miles from Paris and dominated an open plateau that offered favourable terrain for tanks all the way to the French capital.

To varying degrees, numerous D-Day objectives had been achieved, but 21st Army Group's ambitions had come up short. The capture of Caen and the city of Bayeux, cutting the road between them, and seizing Carpiquet airfield, remained. And each was vital to the inland movement of 21st Army Group's divisions and their expected junction with the US V Corps, under the command of General Leonard Gerow.

As General Bernard Montgomery, commander of Allied ground forces in Normandy, maintained his push toward Caen, a desperate battle was brewing there. Hitler had personally retained control of the majority of German armoured reserves in Normandy, and like numerous senior Wehrmacht officers, he believed that landings there were a diversion with the real invasion force to come ashore at the Pas-de-Calais, well to the northeast. German armoured units on the ground were prohibited from counterattacking the Allied beachhead without personal orders from the Führer. In the event, Hitler slept until 10am on June 6, 1944, and only a thrust by tanks of the 21st Panzer Division had moved ahead during the day. Ultimately, 21st Panzer was forced to pull back due to lack of reinforcements.

Finally, late in the afternoon of June 6, the 12th SS Panzer 'Hitler Jugend' and Panzer Lehr divisions were released to fight in Normandy, and the concentration of German armour and Nazi fervour made the battle for Caen a protracted ordeal. By evening on June 6, the 25th Panzergrenadier Regiment, vanguard of the 12th SS, was in

A British soldier takes aim with his Lee Enfield rifle during the battle for Caen. (Collections of the Imperial War Museums via Wikimedia Commons)

An ammunition carrier of the British 11th Armoured Division explodes during Operation Epsom. (United Kingdom Government via Wikimedia Commons)

position to contest the advance on Caen. Its commanding officer, SS Standartenführer (Colonel) Kurt 'Panzer' Meyer, climbed to the top of the belltower at the Abbey of Ardenne on the outskirts of Caen and watched the tanks and troops of the Canadian 3rd Division moving toward Carpiquet airfield.

Meyer muttered: "Little fish! We'll throw them back into the sea in the morning!" On June 7 (D+1), the panzergrenadiers unleashed a counterattack that pushed the Canadians back two miles. Only heavy naval gunfire from offshore halted the Germans, but half Meyer's tanks were destroyed that morning. With only 17 tanks left and preoccupied with holding Caen, Meyer could do little to prevent the British 50th Division from cutting the Bayeux-Caen road. Bayeux fell to the British on June 8, but Caen remained in German control.

Montgomery hammered away at the defenders of Caen, drawing the German armour onto his 21st Army Group and away from the 12th Army Group under General Omar Bradley, fighting to the west and south. On June 10, Montgomery ordered a two-pronged attack by the 7th Armoured Division, the famed Desert Rats of North Africa, moving south and combining with the British 51st Division and 4th Armoured Brigade, also sweeping south from positions east of the River Orne. Focusing on Hill 112, a commanding position just south of Carpiquet, the pincer movement was blunted by a 21st Panzer counterattack. However, the

Germans of the 12th SS Panzer Division Hitlerjugend are shown aboard a reconnaissance vehicle in the ruins of Caen. (National Digital Archives of Poland via Wikimedia Commons)

Soldiers of the 43rd Wessex Division take cover as German mortar fire erupts near Caen. (United Kingdom Government via Wikimedia Commons)

7th Division spearhead stretched around the enemy flank toward the town of Villers-Bocage and threatened the rear of Panzer Lehr.

Despite the progress, disaster struck on June 13, when SS Hauptsturmführer (Captain) Michael Wittman and elements of the 101st SS Heavy Tank Battalion mauled the 4th County of London Yeomanry and the 1st Battalion Rifle Brigade while it was halted along the national highway at the crest of Hill 213 at Villers-Bocage. Twenty-five British tanks and 28 other armoured vehicles were destroyed, most of them by Wittman's 56-ton Tiger tanks with their 88mm cannon.

The fighting for Caen, however, continued virtually without pause. Elements of both Panzer Lehr and the 2nd SS Panzer Division Das Reich deployed near Caen and stabilised the front against further attacks through June 22, while the British 11th Armoured Division crashed into the Hitlerjugend near Hill 112 and was stopped again.

As Montgomery's hopes of taking Caen by swift manoeuvre were dashed, the general ordered a major assault. On June 26, Operation Epsom commenced with a heavy artillery barrage and two armoured brigades leading the way. The British finally took Hill 112 on June 28, and a bridgehead was established across the River Odon. However, the introduction of two new panzer divisions, the 9th SS Hohenstaufen and 10th SS Frundsberg, contributed to a successful German counterstroke that brought Epsom to a halt.

On July 8, Montgomery struck again. Operation Charnwood was one of the costliest battles of the campaign in Normandy. British and Canadian troops finally met in the heart of Caen on July 9, after Allied bombers pounded the 12th SS Hitlerjugend with 2,600 tons of bombs and reduced the city to rubble in the process. The 3rd Canadian Division fought weary panzergrenadiers for control of Carpiquet, and the airfield was secured the same day. However, the Allies lost 103 tanks in the fighting.

Less than a week later, Montgomery unleashed Operation Goodwood to capitalize on the gains of Epsom and Charnwood and solidify the Allied grip on Caen. Air and artillery bombardment on a grand scale preceded the British thrust southward toward Bourguebus Ridge, but a quick counterattack by the 1st SS Panzer Division Leibstandarte Adolf Hitler and 21st Panzer Division stopped the British advance. The Germans held the vital ridge for two more days before they were compelled to withdraw. The defenders had suffered heavily, but they had destroyed 500 British and Commonwealth tanks, one-third of Montgomery's armoured strength.

In the days that followed the capture of Caen, the progress of 21st Army Group was slow, but the combat efficiency of the German divisions that had been engaged had been substantially eroded. And to the west, Bradley and 12th Army Group launched Operation Cobra on July 25, achieving a breakthrough that threatened to outflank all the German forces in Normandy.

Above: A British soldier carries a French child through the rubble of Caen after the city's capture. (Collections of the Imperial War Museums via Wikimedia Commons)

Right: Soldiers of the King's Shropshire Light Infantry rest beside a Sherman tank after the city of Caen has been liberated. (Collections of the Imperial War Museums via Wikimedia Commons)

LVOV-SANDOMIERZ OFFENSIVE BEGINS

Launched in support of Operation Bagration, the Red Army offensive in the Lvov and Sandomierz areas aimed to push German forces out of Ukraine and eastern Poland. More than a million troops, 11,000 artillery pieces and nearly 2,000 tanks and armoured vehicles led by Marshal Ivan Konev attacked to liberate the city of Lvov and establish Soviet bridgeheads across the River Vistula.

Heavily outnumbered, German Army Group North Ukraine, under Colonel General Josef Harpe, could field roughly 440,000 soldiers and fewer than 450 tanks and self-propelled assault guns to stem the Soviet onslaught, a two-pronged offensive with the 1st Guards Tank Army, 3rd Guards Army, and 13th Armies striking toward Rava-Ruska while the 38th, 60th, 3rd Guards Tank Army, and 4th Tank Army advanced on Lvov itself.

The Red Army offensive commenced across a narrow front where superiority in troops and firepower were assured. Konev positioned 240 guns spaced roughly every half mile along a 16-mile corridor of advance. By the end of the first day, the German XLII Army Korps

Above: Soviet infantry officers confer during offensive operations on the Eastern Front during 1944. (Archives of the Russian Federation via Wikimedia Commons)

Right: Colonel General Josef Harpe was responsible for defending against the Red Army offensive on Lvov and Sandomierz. (Bundesarchiv Bild via Wikimedia Commons)

had been forced to retreat more than 12 miles before the attacks of the northern thrust. In the south, the assaults directly toward Lvov placed the German XIII Korps in a precarious position near the town of Brody.

Two days later, a weak German counterattack by the understrength 16th and 17th Panzer Divisions was blunted, and those depleted forces compelled to join a general withdrawal. Konev responded by hastening a mobile assault group to the western bank of the Southern Bug River, cutting off the retreat of the entire XIII Korps. Approximately 45,000 German troops were trapped in the subsequent encirclement, and a breach 225 miles wide had been torn in the Wehrmacht front line. Only about one-third of the Germans trapped at Brody managed to reach safety after larger formations were broken down into elements of just a few men to attempt the exfiltration.

Lvov fell to the Red Army on July 28, and after the Germans had been forced completely out of western Ukraine, Stavka, the Soviet high command, issued orders to expand the offensive. Red Army forces were directed to use the Vistula crossings as a springboard for the capture of the town of Sandomierz in southern Poland. Early westward thrusts were met by substantial German counterattacks, bolstered by the eventual transfer of 11 German and three Hungarian divisions along with a battalion of Tiger tanks and three brigades of Sturmgeschütz self-propelled assault guns. The Soviets sustained heavy losses, in some cases their armoured divisions reduced to just a handful of tanks.

Fierce German resistance prevented further Soviet advances, and the front stabilised by the end of August as Stavka deemed the offensive successful, having achieved its objectives via the bridgehead across the Vistula and 75-mile penetration of German lines with the capture of Sandomierz.

Tanks of the Soviet 3rd Guards Tank Army halt in a wooded area during fighting on the Eastern Front. (Archives of Ukraine via Wikimedia Commons)

PRIME MINISTER TOJO RESIGNS

After 33 months in office and having become virtual dictator of the Japanese Empire, Hideki Tojo resigned along with his entire cabinet. The fall of Saipan in the Marianas was the trigger that ended the hawkish run of Tojo and the militarist faction that emerged within the Japanese Army during the 1930s.

A graduate of the Imperial Military Academy and the Military Staff College, Tojo served as an attaché to the German government in Berlin after World War One. He rose to command the 1st Infantry Regiment and then became chief of staff of the Kwantung Army during its aggression against China. His rapid rise was built on both military successes in Manchuria and his stern command presence that earned Tojo the nickname of 'the Razor'.

Tojo became a prime shaper of Japanese foreign policy while serving as vice minister of war and supported the signing of the Tripartite Pact of 1940 with Nazi Germany and Fascist Italy to form the Rome-Berlin-Tokyo Axis. During the ongoing power struggle, Tojo was elevated to the post of minister of war and collided with the more moderate government faction under Prime Minister Prince Fumimaro Konoye. The prime minister resigned in October 1940, and Tojo assumed that office while consolidating his power with the responsibilities of army minister, minister of war, and minister of commerce and industry.

Approving of the bombing of Pearl Harbor, Tojo steadily marched Japan toward all-out war in the Pacific. He promised that Japan would lead a new economic and diplomatic hegemony called the 'Greater East Asia Co-Prosperity Sphere' and either persuaded or coerced the generals and politicians in the government to follow him into the conflict with the United States, Great Britain and its Commonwealth, and other European countries.

Early successes seemed to validate Tojo's militaristic perspective. However, by 1943 the Japanese juggernaut had seen its days of glorious and relatively easy victories evaporate. The Allies had assumed the offensive in the Pacific, and even as Tojo attempted to reinforce his control of the military by assuming the post of

Approaching the height of his power, Prime Minister Hideki Tojo poses with cabinet members in October 1941. (Government of Japan via Wikimedia Commons)

chief of the army general staff, the fortunes of war were turning decidedly against the Axis. Navy Minister Admiral Shigetaro Shimada simultaneously assumed the post of chief of the navy general staff.

In September 1943, the 'Jushin' or 'Senior Statesmen' organised against Tojo, convinced that the war would not end as long as he was in power. The Jushin actually used Tojo's expansion of power to their advantage, pointing out that the military reverses experienced by the Imperial Armed Forces had come under Tojo's leadership. Although he attempted to reorganise his government once again, Tojo lost the confidence of Emperor Hirohito, which doomed his tenure.

The fall of Tojo's government was succeeded by a more moderate regime under General Kuniaki Koiso and Admiral Mitsumasa Yonia. After the war, Tojo was arrested and charged with war crimes. An attempted suicide failed, and he was convicted and hanged in 1948.

Above: The Japanese government under Prime Minister Hideki Tojo fell in July 1944 following a string of military defeats. (Government of Japan via Wikimedia Commons)

Right: Prime Minister Tojo bows before the funeral portrait of Admiral Isoroku Yamamoto in May 1943. (Government of Japan via Wikimedia Commons)

HITLER ASSASSINATION ATTEMPT FAILS

On July 20, 1944 Adolf Hitler survived the powerful blast of a bomb planted at Wolf's Lair, his headquarters near the small town of Rastenburg in East Prussia, and the survival reinforced his conviction of his personal destiny that is intertwined with the eventual victory of the Third Reich in World War Two.

Several earlier assassination attempts had failed during the years of Hitler's political prominence. Among these was the November 8, 1939, bombing of the Bürgerbräukeller in Munich, where Hitler addressed a crowd on the anniversary of the failed 1923 Beer Hall Putsch and left the rostrum 13 minutes before the explosive, planted by dissident Georg Elser, detonated, killing eight and wounding 62. Hitler managed to survive or thwart numerous assassination attempts by changing schedules abruptly, altering plans, surrounding himself with protective bodyguards, or somehow achieving a political or military triumph that at least temporarily endeared him to the people.

However, by the summer of 1944, even the Führer's good fortune had waned appreciably. Germany was losing the war on all fronts, and Hitler's health had deteriorated noticeably. He ranted frequently, issued orders that were without military merit, and at times seemed to be detached from reality. The situation was not lost on Generals Henning von Tresckow, chief of staff of the Second Army on the Eastern Front, and Friedrich Olbricht, a senior staff officer in Berlin. These conspirators led a group of high-ranking army officers, anti-Nazi politicians, and former government officials who were convinced that the war was irretrievably lost, and the only option was to sue for peace. Field Marshal Erwin Rommel, the famed Desert Fox, was an immensely popular figure in Germany and also quietly involved in the plot.

The conspirators concluded that Hitler was their greatest obstacle, and that the Führer had to be eliminated. The plot to kill Hitler took shape early in 1944, and at its centre was Lieutenant Colonel Klaus von Stauffenberg, a decorated combat veteran of the North African campaign during which he had been grievously wounded,

Reichsmarschall Hermann Göring and German officers inspect the bombed conference room at Wolf's Lair. (Bundesarchiv Bild via Wikimedia Commons)

losing his left eye, right hand, and two fingers of his left hand in action. Stauffenberg had been appointed chief of staff to General Friedrich Fromm, commander of the Home Army in Berlin, and regularly attended Hitler's daily briefings on the rapidly worsening military situation.

Stauffenberg volunteered to carry a powerful bomb concealed in his briefcase into the briefing at Wolf's Lair on July 20. With Hitler dead, an edict called Operation Valkyrie would be activated in Berlin. The army would take control of the government, arresting or detaining senior Nazis, leaders of the SS, and army officers who were hostile, thereby depriving any resistance to the coup d'etat substantive organisational leadership. Similar moves were to be made across Germany and occupied Europe.

On the appointed day, Stauffenberg entered the briefing room and placed the bomb under the heavy oak table close to Hitler's position. Excusing himself, Stauffenberg walked briskly from the briefing room. However, another officer unknowingly moved the briefcase behind a heavy leg of the oak table, and when the bomb detonated Hitler was shielded from the primary force of the blast. Four men were killed and 13 injured. Stauffenberg witnessed the explosion and was sure Hitler was dead.

Bluffing his way through a roadblock, Stauffenberg exited the Wolf's Lair compound and immediately flew back to Berlin expecting Operation Valkyrie to be in motion along with the public announcement of Hitler's death. But nothing had been done as other officers waited for independent

Far left: Lieutenant Colonel Claus von Stauffenberg is shown at left with another officer in June 1944. (Selbst European Union via Wikimedia Commons)

Left: Stauffenberg is shown at far left in the presence of Hitler at Wolf's Lair five days before the July 20 bombing. (Bundesarchiv Bild via Wikimedia Commons)

him to suppress the coup attempt. Within hours, the plot had come apart. Stauffenberg and several other conspirators were cornered, placed under arrest, and summarily shot without trial.

Although he received some burns, an arm was stiffened, and he was somewhat deafened by the explosion, Hitler greeted Benito Mussolini upon his arrival at a train station near Wolf's Lair that afternoon. He showed his visiting comrade the shredded pants he had been wearing at the time of the blast and spoke with conviction about his destiny, that fate had once again spared him for even greater achievement. At 1am on July 21, 1944, the Führer spoke to the German people: "German national comrades! Yet another of the countless attempts on my life has been planned and carried out…I have to continue my work and therefore I will continue it."

In the wake of the assassination attempt, Hitler exacted terrible vengeance. More than 7,000 people were arrested, and numerous show trials were held with nearly 5,000 people found guilty of some form of treason and executed in a gruesome manner. Many of the grisly executions were filmed for Hitler to view later.

The failed July 20 assassination attempt contributed further to the decline of Hitler's physical and mental stability. In less than a year, the Third Reich was crumbling around him, and he took his own life.

Left: Hitler was wearing these shredded trousers at the time of the blast at Wolf's Lair on July 20, 1944. (Bundesarchiv Bild via Wikimedia Commons)

Right: A leader in the July 20, 1944, assassination plot against Hitler, General Henning von Tresckow later committed suicide. (Bundesarchiv Bild via Wikimedia Commons)

Below: German soldiers mill about in the area where several of the July 20 conspirators were summarily shot by firing squad. (Bundesarchiv Bild via Wikimedia Commons)

confirmation of the Führer's demise. Stauffenberg was dumbfounded as precious time had slipped away.

Meanwhile, Major Otto Remer raced to the office of Propaganda Minister Josef Goebbels to comply with Valkyrie orders and place the minister under arrest. Remer was astonished to find that Hitler was very much alive. Goebbels in fact allowed him to speak directly to the Führer by telephone. Hitler promoted Remer to colonel and ordered

US FORCES LAND ON GUAM

When US troops landed on the beaches of Guam on July 21, 1944, many of them were veterans of the hard fighting on Bougainville in 1943. The Marines and US Army troops of the III Amphibious Corps were comprised of the 3rd Marine Division, the artillery of the 12th Marine Regiment, the engineers of the 19th Marine Regiment, the 1st Provisional Marine Brigade, and the Army's 77th Infantry Division.

The southernmost and largest island of the Marianas archipelago with an area of 209 sq miles, Guam is a US territorial possession that had fallen to the Japanese on December 10, 1941, the third day of World War Two in the Pacific. Three weeks of combat followed the initial Marine and Army landings, but by August 10 most organised enemy resistance has ended.

Unlike the interservice angst that characterised operations on Saipan, the Marines praised their army comrades of the 77th Infantry Division, who proudly wore the Statue of Liberty shoulder flash since most of the recruits and draftees hailed from New York City when the division was formed a generation earlier during the Great War. The Marines actually bestowed upon the army troops the moniker of the '77th Marine Division'.

Altogether the US forces poised to take Guam numbered well over 50,000 under the command of Marine General Roy S. Geiger of III Amphibious Corps, while the 3rd Marine Division was led by General Allan H. 'Hal' Turnage, the 1st Provisional Marine Brigade by General Lemuel C. Shepherd, Jr., and the 77th Division by General Andrew D. Bruce. The opposing Japanese forces numbered roughly 18,500, primarily of the 29th Infantry Division, the 48th Independent Mixed Brigade, and the 10th Independent Mixed Regiment under the command of General Hideyoshi Obata and tactically led by General Takeshi Takashina of the 29th Division.

Early fighting on Guam was heavy, but at the end of the first day the Marines had advanced inland more than 2,000 yards in some areas. Twenty-four landing craft of the 22nd Marines, 1st Provisional Marine Brigade were destroyed during the assault at Gaan Point in the south, where the Japanese had placed a pair of 75mm guns and a 37mm gun in concrete reinforced blockhouses that had withstood the preinvasion naval bombardment. The enemy positions were finally enveloped from the rear and silenced. Bitter subsequent fighting also took place at Bundschu Ridge, named for Captain Geary Bundschu who was killed early in the battle for Guam, and at Hill 40.

After landing and securing its beachhead, the 77th Infantry Division began a northward movement that linked up beachheads from north to south on the island. A joint advance of Marines and US Army troops recaptured the old Marine barracks and the airfield on the Orote Peninsula. On the morning of July 31, General Geiger authorised the final push north with the 3rd Marine Division on the left and the 77th Division on the right.

By the time hostilities ceased, General Obata had committed ritual suicide, and 11,000 Japanese were dead. The remainder, some hiding in caves for months, were killed or taken prisoner during the next year. Nearly 1,600 Marines were killed on Guam and 5,000 wounded, while the 77th Infantry Division lost 177 dead and 662 wounded.

Officers of the 77th Infantry Division plant the US flag on Guam in the Marianas. (US Army via Wikimedia Commons)

US Marines move inland during the fighting on Guam in the Marianas Islands. (US Navy via Wikimedia Commons)

Japanese prisoners captured on Guam bow their heads upon hearing of the empire's 1945 surrender. (US Army via Wikimedia Commons)

Knocked out PzKpfw. IV and PzKpfw. VI Tiger tanks of the Panzer Lehr Division lie abandoned in Normandy. (Bundesarchiv Bild via Wikimedia Commons)

OPERATION COBRA: NORMANDY BREAKOUT

Hundreds of Allied bombers pounded an area three and one-half miles wide and a half-mile deep along the German front in Normandy, stunning the defenders such as to render them incapable of resisting an immediate surge of the US 4th, 9th, and 30th Infantry Divisions plunging through the area of saturation bombing to hold open the shoulders of the newly established breakthrough.

Following rapidly behind the infantry divisions, the US 2nd and 3rd Armored Divisions and the motorised 1st Infantry Division exploited the gap and raced toward the town of Coutances. Operation Cobra, the Allied breakout from the Normandy beachhead was underway.

Generals Omar Bradley (left) and J. Lawton Collins confer near the French city of Cherbourg. (US Army via Wikimedia Commons)

After weeks of fighting in Normandy, Allied progress from the D-Day lodgement had been generally sluggish. Although the US VII Corps of General Omar Bradley's 12th Army Group had captured the port of Cherbourg, that accomplishment occurred two weeks behind schedule. At the same time, the 21st Army Group under General Bernard Montgomery, hammered away at the city of Caen, a D-Day objective, and did not secure the communications and transportation centre until July 9.

A Stuart light tank of the US 4th Armored Division advances toward Coutances during Operation Cobra. (US Department of Defense via Wikimedia Commons)

Left: General Lesley McNair was accidentally killed during the Operation Cobra saturation bombing. (US Army Signal Corps via Wikimedia Commons)

Right: General George S. Patton, Jr., commander of the US Third Army, salutes while standing in a Jeep. (US Army via Wikimedia Commons)

Tenacious German resistance had been incapable of throwing the Allies back into the English Channel, but several powerful counterattacks had managed to stabilise the front in Normandy. Further, the hedgerow country, or bocage, impeded an overall advance in the west due to its high, earthen mounds, hundreds of years old, that stretched for miles with drainage ditches alongside. The hedgerows were several feet thick with trees growing atop them, many more than 20ft high. The bocage was perfect ambush country, and the Germans defended every country lane and field.

After the fall of Cherbourg, General Bradley reoriented the bulk of First Army to the south with two major objectives, the crossroads town of Saint Lo on the eastern flank, and the village of Coutances, where five roads converged 15 miles to the west. Stiff resistance stalled the offensive that jumped off on July 3, 1944, even as the majority of the German armoured forces in Normandy continued to battle Montgomery's forces in the area around Caen.

Bradley, however, had already been contemplating Operation Cobra, a sledgehammer blow that would literally blast an opening in the German lines. Bad weather impeded the start of Cobra, and there were two unfortunate incidents of friendly fire that killed more than 130 American troops and wounded dozens of others. Among the dead was General Lesley McNair, commander of US Army Ground Forces.

When the offensive did get underway on July 25, waves of 2,350 heavy and medium bombers dropped 4,000 tons of bombs on positions occupied by the German LXXXIV Korps, under General Dietrich von Choltitz, consisting of the remnants of several infantry divisions already decimated in the Normandy fighting, as well as the 2nd SS Panzer Division Das Reich, Panzer Lehr, and the 17th SS Panzergrenadier Division. Panzer Lehr was in the centre of the maelstrom and at the time could muster only 2,200 troops and 45 tanks and armoured vehicles, a shadow of its original strength of 15,000 troops and 200 tanks.

General Fritz Beyerlein, commander of Panzer Lehr, observed the results of the saturation bombing with horror. "The shock effect on the troops was indescribable," he wrote later. "Several of my men went mad and rushed around in the open until they were cut down by splinters. Simultaneously with the storm from the air, innumerable guns of the American artillery poured drumfire into our field positions."

Panzer Lehr suffered 1,000 killed or wounded in the aerial onslaught.

When the spearheads of the VII Corps moved out, many using the Saint Lo-Periers Road as an initial route of advance, one battalion of the 330th Infantry Regiment raced forward 800 yards in just 40 minutes. However, once the Germans shook off their torpor, heavy resistance slowed the advance toward the afternoon of July 25. At the end of the day, the average penetration of the German line was about two miles, well short of expectations. Bradley retained an optimistic perspective and reassured other senior officers that the going was always slower than hoped in the early hours of a ground offensive.

Bradley's optimism was rewarded during the next 48 hours. By the evening of July 27, he told General Dwight Eisenhower, supreme commander of Allied forces, "Things look really good." Bradley prodded his corps commanders to "maintain unrelenting pressure" on the Germans, who were falling back to avoid possible encirclement in some areas. A major effort to capture Coutances and trap thousands of German soldiers between the advancing US VII and VIII Corps was pressed.

On August 1, the recently arrived US Third Army, under the command of hard-driving General George S. Patton, Jr., became operational, and Bradley gave VIII Corps to the aggressive combat leader ahead of a scheduled transfer. Therefore, Patton pre-emptively ordered the 4th and 6th Armored Divisions to race through the Cobra breach toward Coutances. The town fell to elements of the 4th Armored Division on July 28.

Without appreciable pause, Patton slashed toward Avranches in the south, the gateway to Brittany where crossings of the River See would place American armoured spearheads in open country, free of the hedgerows, and poised to dash across France. Meanwhile, resistance was relatively light as German soldiers surrendered in large numbers. Avranches was undefended when US tanks rolled along its streets on the 30th.

From there, VIII Corps turned west and drove 200 miles to liberate the port of Brest in less than a week. In eight days, Patton's tanks had swept through Le Mans and were halfway to Paris. By the time the Third Army juggernaut was halted by a lack of fuel and supplies at the end of the month, Patton's command had covered 400 miles and liberated 50,000 sq miles of French territory while taking thousands of German prisoners. At the same time, a further devastating defeat loomed for the Germans at Falaise.

US tanks and troops enter the city of Coutances, France, during Operation Cobra. (US Army via Wikimedia Commons)

WARSAW UPRISING BEGINS

Encouraged by the approach of the Soviet Red Army, which had already ejected the Nazis from much of eastern Poland, the Home Army in Warsaw rose up in open rebellion against the Nazis in the evening of August 1. Under the command of General Tadeusz Bor-Komorowski, the uprising began with the approval of the democratic Polish government-in-exile in London in hopes that the liberation of the city would occur prior to the arrival of the Red Army. The Soviets had already established their own communist-led Polish Committee of National Liberation in areas under their control.

While the German garrison of Warsaw was relatively weak, the 50,000 strong Home Army made notable gains in the early days of the uprising. Although it was poorly armed and equipped, food shortages were persistent, and medical care for the wounded was virtually absent, there was some expectation that the Soviets would provide relief in the form of direct aid along with offensive efforts to reach the capital and support the fight against the common Nazi enemy.

In the event, though, Soviet Premier Josef Stalin ordered the Red Army spearheads to halt in the suburbs of Warsaw on the opposite bank of the River Vistula, thereby allowing German forces to subdue the Home Army, which constituted the only substantial obstacle to the establishment of a pro-Soviet government throughout liberated Poland. While declining to directly intervene in the fighting, the Soviets denied the Western Allies access to airfields that would facilitate a resupply effort by air, including humanitarian aid for thousands of civilians caught up in the conflict.

After three days of fighting, the Home Army had driven the Germans from most of Warsaw, taking control of transportation and communication centres. The fighting was savage, and one teenager who fought the Nazis remembered a special enmity for the SS troops that had wantonly murdered and brutalised the citizenry of Warsaw, particularly the Jews who had risen against their occupiers in early 1943.

"Positioned immediately under the window from which I was firing was an SS police machine gun squad," the fighter recalled. "At the first burst from Cadet Officer Zawada's Sten gun a machine gunner was shot down. Although he was badly wounded, he tried to retreat, spitting blood and leaving a deadly red trail on the pavement. A rifle shot finished him off…We did not spare ammunition when shooting at the SS policemen – the men who had been responsible for the slaughter in the Ghetto, for the executions, the street hunts, and the wanton murders."

The Home Army attacked the state telephone exchange building in the city, using improvised explosives and jury-rigged flamethrowers to oust the Germans. Fighters moved through the sewers and set booby traps for the unsuspecting enemy. One group managed to capture a German tank and used it to plough through the rubble of the Jewish ghetto and free about 400 inmates in a detention camp.

Adolf Hitler flew into a rage when news of the uprising reached Berlin. The Nazi response was swift, and by mid-August a ruthless campaign to exterminate the Home Army and reduce the city to rubble was underway. Reichsführer SS Heinrich Himmler unleashed massive firepower against the rebelling Poles and made a dire prediction: "Warsaw will be liquidated, and this city which has blocked our path to the east for 700 years will have ceased to exist."

On August 25, 1944, the Germans launched a major counterattack that included

Right: General Tadeusz Bor-Komorowski commanded the Home Army during the 1944 Warsaw uprising. (Republic of Poland via Wikimedia Commons)

Below: Flames consume the Old Town district of Warsaw during the suppression of the uprising by Nazi troops in 1944. (Ewa Faryaszewska Museum of Warsaw via Wikimedia Commons)

Fighters of the Home Army drive a captured German halftrack through a Warsaw street during the 1944 uprising. (Republic of Poland via Wikimedia Commons)

Troops of the Polish Home Army are shown with their unit's standard in Warsaw. (Republic of Poland via Wikimedia Commons)

reinforcing Wehrmacht and SS troops along with former Soviet prisoners who had either been coerced or volunteered to fight with the Nazis. German aircraft bombed and strafed, while tanks rumbled through the streets of Warsaw, blasting positions believed occupied by Home Army rebels. The combat was often street to street and building to building, and control of some structures changed hands several times. All the while, the Germans murdered indiscriminately, killing civilians, including women and children, without respite.

Although the overwhelming German superiority in firepower forced the Home Army to assume a defensive posture, the uprising persisted well beyond its intended short duration of only about 10 days. The rebels were squeezed into an ever-tightening pocket in the Old Town section of Warsaw. The destruction was pervasive, but some fighters held on grimly while others broke up into small groups and managed to make their way out of the embattled city.

Only in mid-September, after the majority of the Home Army had been killed, wounded, or captured, did Stalin allow some relief to be delivered to the people who remained in the shattered city. Finally, after 63 days the remnants of the rebel force laid down their arms. An estimated 15,000 fighters of the Home Army and 250,000 civilians were killed in the tragedy of the uprising, while the Germans sustained about 16,000 casualties.

The Red Army entered Warsaw in January 1945, and subsequently a Soviet puppet regime was established in Poland with the acquiescence of the Western Allied powers which ostensibly gained some "sphere of influence" concessions elsewhere.

A fighter of the Home Army armed with a flamethrower peers around a corner during the uprising. (Republic of Poland via Wikimedia Commons)

German soldiers advance against the Home Army in Warsaw's Theatre Square, 1944. (Bundesarchiv Bild via Wikimedia Commons)

OPERATION DRAGOON: ALLIES INVADE SOUTHERN FRANCE

Nine weeks after the D-Day landings in Normandy, Allied troops came ashore in France once again, this time along the southern coast. Operation Dragoon included two armies, the US Seventh and French Army B, under General Alexander M. Patch and General Jean de Lattre de Tassigny, respectively. The Dragoon landings played a significant role in the Allied offensive in western Europe. General Dwight Eisenhower, supreme commander of Allied forces, needed another major port to supply his armies in their drive toward the frontier of the Third Reich, while a second thrust in France would press the enemy between two vast Allied forces, bring more troops into France before winter set in, and introduce large numbers of French soldiers into the fight to liberate their homeland.

An Allied naval armada lies offshore during Operation Dragoon, the invasion of southern France. (US Navy via Wikimedia Commons)

Originally codenamed Operation Anvil, the landings were renamed due to security concerns. Allied airborne forces were slated to land by parachute and glider to seize points inland from the invasion beaches, while French commandos came ashore along a 35-mile stretch of the Riviera between the cities of Cannes and Toulon. A powerful fleet of four aircraft carriers, six battleships, 21 cruisers, and scores of destroyers added air cover and preinvasion artillery bombardment.

The German 19th Army, under General Friedrich Weise, defended southern France. These troops included seven divisions, but three of them were static coastal formations of dubious fighting quality, while many of the troops under Weise were ex-POWs from Russia and Poland who opted to fight for Germany rather than languish in

American troops and tanks pause on the shoreline in southern France during Operation Dragoon. (Government of France via Wikimedia Commons)

a stalag. Only one panzer division, the 11th, was available, roughly at half strength with 14,000 grenadiers and fewer than 100 tanks.

Just before 8am, the first US troops of General Lucian Truscott's VI Corps, splashed ashore. Immediate opposition was generally light, but a pitched battle occurred in one sector of the beachhead labelled 'Camel Red'. Within hours, soldiers from shore linked up with airborne units, and the cities of Le Muy and Saint-Tropez were in American hands. The French came ashore and turned toward Toulon and Marseilles. The cities fell to de Tassigny's command on August 27 and 28. The French sustained 4,500 casualties and captured 11,000 prisoners.

In the coming days, the American 36th Division liberated Grenoble in the French Alps and Lyon six weeks ahead of schedule. The French rolled up the valley of the River Rhone, entered Dijon, and joined up with General George S. Patton's Third Army. In less than a month, Patch's Seventh Army had advanced 500 miles.

Retreating German forces were in fact squeezed within the vice of Allied armies advancing from Normandy and the Riviera. Huge quantities of supplies, meanwhile, were being offloaded at Marseilles and Toulon. Operation Dragoon, therefore, played a key role in the Allied victory in western Europe.

German soldiers man an 88mm anti-aircraft gun on a beach in southern France. (Bundesarchiv Bild via Wikimedia Commons)

ALLIES REACH GOTHIC LINE IN ITALY

Two months after the liberation of Rome, the Allied Fifth and Eighth Armies drew up to the fortifications of the Gothic Line, the last prepared line of German defences in Italy. By August 1944, the Germans had been conducting a static defence or fighting retreat in Italy for two years, and the Todt Organization, the paramilitary construction arm of the Nazi government, had been planning and building the defences since mid-1943.

The Gothic Line stretched 200 miles across the northern Apennine Mountains from the naval base at La Spezia on the Ligurian Sea in the west to the Foglia Valley and the port of Pesaro on the Adriatic Sea in the east. By the time the Allies arrived, the Gothic Line consisted of 2,400 machine-gun positions and 500 mortar and artillery emplacements, some of these reinforced in concrete bunkers and pillboxes. Todt workers had strung nearly 75 miles of barbed wire, and numerous turrets mounting 75mm guns taken from PzKpfw. V Panther tanks had been mounted on concrete and steel bases.

Field Marshal Albert Kesselring, commanding German forces in the Italian theatre, hoped to defend the Gothic Line to deny the Allies access to the Valley of the River Po that lay some distance beyond. The gateway to the Po Valley, good tank country with firm ground for armoured vehicles, was the city of Bologna, while Modena and Milan were also key objectives. Possession of the rich farm country would also deprive the Germans of a major food source. Further, Allied senior officers, Field Marshal Sir Harold Alexander, commanding Allied armies in Italy, General Sir Oliver Leese, commanding Eighth Army,

British soldiers of the 5th Battalion, Sherwood Foresters, advance toward the Gothic Line accompanied by an M10 tank destroyer. (Collections of the Imperial War Museums via Wikimedia Commons)

Above: Polish soldiers inspect a captured German PzKpfw. V Panther tank near the Gothic Line. (Republic of Poland via Wikimedia Commons)

Left: After the breach of the Gothic Line, Brazilian soldiers of the Allied Fifth Army advance toward Bologna. (Government of Brazil via Wikimedia Commons)

and General Mark W. Clark, commanding Fifth Army, wanted to advance as far as possible before winter.

Eighth Army renewed its offensive in the east on August 25 as V Corps and the 1st Canadian Corps forced the German LXXVI Panzer Korps and LI Mountain Korps back into the Gothic Line defences. Soon, Leese was in position to outflank the static fortifications at Pesaro, and by September 3 the stunning advance had accomplished the task while capturing 4,000 prisoners. Although Eighth Army's progress was slowed by stubborn resistance at Coriano Ridge, the city of Rimini was taken on September 21.

Meanwhile, Clark's spearheads crossed the River Arno at Florence and drove smartly into the centre of the Gothic Line 20 miles to the north. Pisa fell on September 2, and by the end of the month American troops had seized the tactically vital Futa and Giogo passes on their route toward Bologna. Bad weather set in on the heels of the Allied successes, and an autumn of limited gains ensued. Bologna fell on April 21, 1945, and the Allies entered the Po Valley. German forces in Italy surrendered eight days later.

RED ARMY REACHES EAST PRUSSIA BORDER

After more than three years of costly fighting and having sustained millions of casualties, the Soviet Red Army reached the border of East Prussia, the cradle of traditional German militarism. The continuation of Operation Bagration, the summer offensive of 1944, had yielded outstanding results and thus far inflicted on the Nazis one of the largest defeats in German military history. Now, Soviet forces were poised to invade German territory, bringing the ravages of war to the region and wreaking vengeance on the enemy, both its dwindling military complex and its civilian population, for prior Nazi brutality in occupied Soviet territory.

Alluding to the fighting a generation earlier during the Great War, the *New York Times* reported in its August 18 edition: "Russian troops for the first time in thirty years carried the war to the German border yesterday, smashing across a battlefield littered with Nazi dead, burned-out tanks and battered gun platforms and reaching the East Prussian frontier along the Sesupe River in western Lithuania."

During Operation Bagration, the Red Army's 3rd Belorussian Front (army group), under the command of General Ivan Chernyakhovsky, had previously spearheaded the drive toward Minsk, capital of Belorussia, while rupturing the German defensive line of the 3rd and 4th Panzer Armies. After liberating Minsk, Chernyakovsky pressed his army group forward to Vilnius, the capital of Lithuania. During the next two weeks, the 3rd Belorussian Front secured a crossing of the River Nieman and captured the Lithuanian city of Kaunas while moving further west.

The Reuters news service flashed a report to London that described

This commemorative stamp from Belarus celebrates the achievements of the 3rd Belorussian Front in World War Two. (Post of Belarus via Wikimedia Commons)

Left: Pictured in 1943, General Ivan Chernyakhovsky led the 3rd Belorussian Front to great victories. (Russian Federation via Wikimedia Commons)

Below: General Ivan Chernyakhovsky and Red Army officers confer during an offensive against the Nazis. (Mil.ru Ministry of Defence of the Russian Federation via Wikimedia Commons)

the rapidly deteriorating situation for the Germans on the Eastern Front. "Russian troops have fought their way into the Lithuanian frontier station of Virbalis, only three miles from Eydtkuhnen, first town inside the East Prussian border. Reporting this, Reuters' Moscow correspondent says Russian artillery is sending the first shells into German traffic on Hitler's super-highways leading to the frontier, and heavy Soviet forces are now approaching the border from at least six directions. The Stockholm (Sweden) correspondent of the British United Press quotes a radio report that goes as far as to say that the Red Army has already invaded East Prussia via Eydtkuhnen, which is on the Kaunas-Konigsberg railway, and Lyck, farther south…where the German News Agency admits the Russians have broken through the German lines."

By early October, General Chernyakhovsky and the 3rd Belorussian Front were poised to launch the initial Red Army offensive into East Prussia, preparing the way for the final massive Red Army assault on the Third Reich in early 1945.

BATTLE OF FALAISE ENDS

Although belatedly, the pincers of the Allied thrusts to bottle up the remnants of the German Seventh and Fifth Panzer Armies in Normandy had finally closed. Approximately 100,000 German troops with their tanks, armoured vehicles, and heavy weapons had been in danger of being trapped in the Falaise Pocket. Eventually, thousands of enemy prisoners were taken, but many others escaped the encirclement, and while Falaise was indeed a great victory, some of its lustre was lost.

General Omar Bradley, commander of the Allied 12th Army Group, called the Falaise encirclement "…An opportunity that comes to a commander not more than once in a century." Strangely, Adolf Hitler had contributed to the deteriorating predicament, playing directly into Allied hands. Reacting to the American breakout from Normandy accomplished with Operation Cobra, Hitler ordered that all German panzer units in Normandy to concentrate for a swift counterattack dubbed Operation Lüttich. Although Field Marshal Gunther von Kluge, commanding German forces in Normandy, was stupefied by the order, he complied.

Lüttich spluttered to a halt in the face of dogged Allied resistance, particularly at Hill 314, high ground near the French town of Mortain, where the US 2nd Battalion, 120th Infantry Regiment held against repeated assaults. In launching the abortive counterattack, the Germans left avenues of approach open for an encirclement that would have catastrophic consequences.

Generals Dwight Eisenhower, supreme commander of Allied forces in Europe, Bradley, and General Bernard Montgomery, ground forces commander and leader of 21st Army Group, realised that the Germans were vulnerable to being cut off as the Canadian First Army was positioned to the north, the British Second Army to the northwest, the US Third Army to the south, and the US First Army to the west.

Eisenhower issued orders for elements of Third Army, under General George S. Patton, Jr., to turn north from their advance at Le Mans toward Argentan while the British and Canadian armies would attack south from Caen toward Falaise to slam the door on the enemy in Normandy. Patton ordered the XV Corps under General Wade Haislip to slash toward Argentan, and little opposition was encountered. As the first American tanks and troops reached Argentan on August 12, Patton urged that his spearhead should be allowed to continue northward, closing the gap on its own.

However, Bradley had issued strict orders that Patton proceed no further than Argentan. His reasoning has been questioned by historians, but he believed that XV Corps would have been stretched too thinly to hold a line any lengthier than the original objective. Bradley was firm and responded to Patton's overtures with the famous quip, "I preferred a solid shoulder at Argentan to the possibility of a broken neck at Falaise."

Meanwhile, the Canadian First Army, under General Henry Crerar, had jumped off for Falaise on August 7 and made early progress. Within 48 hours, though, the thrust lost momentum as the Canadians met stiff opposition and halted to deal with every centre of German resistance. The 4th Canadian and 1st Polish Armoured Divisions were slowed to a crawl and had made only half the distance to Falaise by August 9.

While Patton was apoplectic, raging for the opportunity to close the Falaise Pocket himself, the Canadians and Poles mounted another surge toward the town of Falaise on August 14. After smashing into

German soldiers captured during the fight toward Falaise are marched away with their hands in the air. (Library and Archives of Canada via Wikimedia Commons)

Ground crewmen service a Hawker Typhoon, one of the Allied fighter-bomber types that devastated the Germans in the Falaise Pocket. (United Kingdom Government via Wikimedia Commons)

A British Cromwell tank passes an abandoned German field artillery piece during the advance toward Falaise. (Collections of the Imperial War Museums via Wikimedia Commons)

In the aftermath of an RAF fighter-bomber attack, the wreckage of a German column is strewn along a roadway in the Falaise Pocket. (Collections of the Imperial War Museums via Wikimedia Commons)

After surrendering at Falaise, German prisoners receive tea from their British captors. (Collections of the Imperial War Museums via Wikimedia Commons)

defensive positions. At the same time, continual air attacks from RAF and US Army Air Forces fighter-bombers ravaged the Germans during daylight hours. The destruction and loss of life were stunning. The Germans had been squeezed into a pocket that was only six to seven miles across at its widest point. There was literally nowhere to hide.

One German soldier caught in the crucible remembered, "We were alive, but inside dead, numbed by watching the horrible scenes which rolled past on both sides." The German defence of Normandy had been undertaken with roughly 50 effective combat divisions. With the debacle of Falaise the campaign ended in decisive defeat, and only the equivalent of 10 divisions remained in the field. About 10,000 Germans were killed in action, while another 40,000 were marched into captivity.

General Eisenhower visited the area soon after the fighting had ended. He was aghast at the devastation and wrote in *Crusade in Europe*, his postwar memoir: "The battlefield at Falaise was unquestionably one of the greatest 'killing fields' of any of the war areas. Forty-eight hours after the closing of the gap I was conducted through it on foot, to encounter scenes that could be described only by Dante. It was literally possible to walk for hundreds of yards at a time, stepping on nothing but dead and decaying flesh."

the Germans with 250 tanks, they reached the objective that day, and Falaise finally fell on August 16. Still, the encirclement was incomplete as a gap of roughly 15 miles remained. While the severely depleted 12th SS Panzer Hitlerjugend and 1st SS Leibstandarte Adolf Hitler Divisions fought like lions to keep the gap open, nearly 50,000 German troops managed to withdraw to the east across the River Dives. Many of these would reorganise and refit as they were able and oppose future Allied operations in The Netherlands and across the frontier of the Third Reich.

Finally, on August 20, Polish, Canadian, and American forces made contact at Chambois to complete the encirclement of the Germans in the Falaise Pocket.

Despite what might have been, Falaise was a disaster for the German armed forces in Normandy. While they fought to survive, the Germans were ravaged by incessant Allied artillery fire, which devastated

General Dwight D. Eisenhower walks beside the overturned chassis of a German PzKpfw. VI Tiger tank blasted by an Allied bomb in the Falaise Pocket. (Acme News Photos US Government via Wikimedia Commons)

ROMANIAN DEFENCES CRUMBLE

By August 23, the Axis government of Romania was on the verge of collapse as the Soviet Red Army renewed its offensive in the northeast of the country. The Soviets had occupied Iasi after breaking through enemy defensive lines, prompting King Michael to order the arrest of Marshal Ion Antonescu, who had served as prime minister and leader of the pro-Nazi Romanian government since 1940.

Three weeks after the break with the Nazis and the Axis, an armistice was concluded on September 12; however, a formal peace treaty between Romania and the Allied nations was not signed until 1947. During the waning months of World War Two, the country actually switched sides and fought with the Allies for the remainder of the conflict. The move deprived Nazi Germany, once and for all, of any vital oil resources from the fields at Ploesti.

Romania had come under fascist influence during the 1930s, and Antonescu, a known anti-Semite, moved the country into the Axis orbit and solidified control over the government serving as his own foreign minister and defence minister. Although King Carol II had dissolved the right-wing government in 1938, aware that laws against the Jews were characteristic of a government similar to that of the Third Reich, he could not contain the pro-Nazi movement.

An opportunistic Soviet Union took advantage of the turmoil in Romania in June 1940, annexing two formerly Romanian provinces and paving the way for the country to align with Germany, fascist Italy, and Imperial Japan. King Carol abdicated the throne a month after the Soviet land grab, allowing Antonescu to assume complete control.

After the Nazi invasion of the Soviet Union on June 22, 1941, Romania temporarily regained control of its lost provinces; however, the Germans plundered the resources of the country, particularly its oil, to fuel their war machine. When the war turned against the Nazis

Romanian Marshal Ion Antonescu greets Nazi Foreign Minister Joachim von Ribbentrop during a conference. (Bundesarchiv Bild via Wikimedia Commons)

and Antonescu sought Western influence to prevent a takeover by the communists, King Michael, son of the deceased Carol, had Antonescu detained. Michael concluded the armistice with the Allies, but in the post-war political environment found it impossible to maintain a Western focus. Michael led the puppet government in the Soviet sphere until his forced abdication in 1947.

Captured by the Soviets, Antonescu was interrogated and held at the notorious Lubyanka Prison in Moscow, where he reportedly attempted suicide. He was later returned to the Romanian capital of Bucharest and was charged with war crimes. He was tried, convicted, and executed along with several others by firing squad on June 1, 1946.

Left: A firing squad ends the life of fascist Romanian leader Ion Antonescu on June 1, 1946. (United States Holocaust Memorial Museum via Wikimedia Commons)

Below: Marshal Ion Antonescu led Romania into a disastrous alliance with Nazi Germany during World War Two. (Republic of Poland via Wikimedia Commons)

LIBERATION OF PARIS

After four years of occupation under the jackboot of the Nazis, Paris, the City of Light and capital of France, was liberated on August 25, 1944. The French 2nd Armoured Division, commanded by General Philippe Leclerc de Hauteclocque reached the city but by the time the division arrives, the French Resistance had already erupted with guerrilla operations, attacking the German garrison, setting up barricades in the streets, and disrupting communications and troop transit.

Free French leader General Charles de Gaulle was instrumental in the decision of General Dwight D. Eisenhower, supreme commander of Allied forces in western Europe, to divert the French formation to Paris. Although the city had no real military significance, de Gaulle was adamant that the French capital should be liberated on humanitarian grounds and threatened to divert the 2nd Armoured Division from Allied control on his own if his demand was not met. De Gaulle also asserted that French troops should be the first into the city to lift the morale of the people.

Despite an order from Adolf Hitler to destroy Paris thoroughly, General Dietrich von Choltitz, commanding the German troops in the city, refused to issue such a diabolical decree. Preferring to surrender rather than go down in history with the stain of the city's destruction as his legacy, Choltitz surrendered to Leclerc and Henri Rol-Tanguy, a communist leader and representative of the French Forces of the Interior, at the Gare Montparnasse, one of several large railway terminals in Paris, in the afternoon. Roughly 5,000 German soldiers laid down their arms.

De Gaulle arrived in the city later the same day, having risen from relative obscurity to lead the French military forces outside the occupied country, forge cooperation among Resistance groups, and repudiate the collaborationist Vichy regime under his former mentor, Marshal Philippe Pétain. De Gaulle had outmanoeuvred his political rival, General Henri Giraud, and assumed authority amid the power vacuum that existed following the fall of France in 1940.

The first stop for General de Gaulle on August 25, 1944, was l'Hotel de Ville, where newsreel cameras whirred and the embodiment of French defiance made his famous declaration, "Paris outraged! Paris broken! Paris martyred! But Paris liberated!" It was a supreme moment of triumph for de Gaulle, but he was perturbed with Leclerc for allowing the communist Rol-Tanguy to join in signing the early surrender documents.

The next day, a million people gathered in the streets of Paris while more Allied troops arrived, and de Gaulle strode down the Champs Élysées in a tumultuous victory parade. Later, he emerged from car at the Cathedral of Notre Dame and strode erect in the midst of sniper fire, undeterred, unflinching, and triumphant as he made his way inside the venerable building.

Above: German General Dietrich von Choltitz signs surrender documents in Paris after four years of Nazi occupation. (Unknown author via Wikimedia Commons)

Left: Fighters of the French Resistance man a barricade during the liberation of Paris, August 25, 1944. (National Museum of the US Navy via Wikimedia Commons)

Below: General Charles de Gaulle leads a victory parade down the Champs Élysées after the liberation of Paris. (Collections of the Imperial War Museums via Wikimedia Commons)

STATE OF WAR
MAY TO AUGUST 1944

On all fronts, the spring and summer of 1944 brought victories for the Allies and continuing setbacks for the Axis.

No one summed up the situation better than Field Marshal Gerd von Rundstedt. When it became apparent that the Allies had returned to northwest Europe to stay and a German counterattack at the end of June turned out to be an exercise in futility, Rundstedt and Field Marshal Wilhelm Keitel, chief of Oberkommando der Wehrmacht (OKW), discussed the situation over the telephone.

Keitel asked what else could be done to remedy the deteriorating situation. Rundstedt replied brusquely, "Make peace, you fools! What else can you do?!" When Adolf Hitler was informed of Rundstedt's comments, it cost the old officer who spoke truth to power his job as commander of German forces in the west. The Führer still nurtured a delusion of victory.

But the walls were closing in on Hitler and the Third Reich.

On July 20, a group of conspirators, among them senior military officers and former government officials, demonstrated the depth of German desperation as Hitler led the nation further into the

Above: With a pair of German prisoners in tow, British soldiers of the 2nd King's Shropshire Light Infantry advance on D-Day. (Collections of the Imperial War Museums via Wikimedia Commons)

Left: American soldiers, tanks, and equipment come ashore in Normandy on D-Day. (Herman V. Wall via Wikimedia Commons)

Below: German prisoners captured during Operation Bagration stream into captivity after the destruction of Army Group Centre. (Unknown Author via Wikimedia Commons)

abyss of defeat and destruction. The bomb blast at Wolf's Lair, Hitler's headquarters in East Prussia, narrowly missed assassinating the Führer. Thousands of people were arrested, many imprisoned, tortured, and summarily executed in Hitler's vengeful response. Most of the core conspirators were shot within hours of the assassination attempt or committed suicide.

From D-Day to the end of August, the Normandy Campaign raged in northern France. After fighting their way ashore on June 6, the

Soviet Red Army soldiers replace a sign in the city of Grodno during Operation Bagration. (Archives of Ukraine via Wikimedia Commons)

Allied armies pushed south and west against stiff German resistance. Although some D-Day objectives were achieved, others proved difficult. General J. Lawton Collins and the US VII Corps captured the French port of Cherbourg at the end of the month, but its facilities were thoroughly wrecked by the Germans. Weeks were required to affect repairs that would allow supply ships to offload there.

Meanwhile, the Germans fought doggedly to hold the city of Caen, just off the French coastline. British General Bernard Montgomery ordered multiple offensive operations to capture Caen, but the city was not firmly in Allied hands until July 9. At the same time, American forces to the west encountered the hedgerow country of Normandy and battled through the farm lanes between the high earthen mounds that separated farmers' fields. The hedgerows, or bocage, were some of the most inhospitable ground for military campaigning in the world. And the Germans contested every yard with hidden machine-gun nests, ambushes, and fortified positions around every corner.

General Omar Bradley, commander of the 12th Army Group, conceived a sledgehammer blow followed by a lightning strike against the German lines that would finally break the defenders and allow Allied forces to dash into Brittany and then across France. On July 25, his Operation Cobra was unleashed. Saturation bombing stunned the enemy, and American armoured and infantry divisions surged through the gap around the French town of St. Lo, and finally there was room to manoeuvre in the open.

Elsewhere in Normandy, at the end of August the German Seventh and Fifth Panzer Armies were in danger of being cut off by converging Allied forces, the American Third Army under General George S. Patton, Jr., reaching Argentan in the south while the Canadian First Army, under General Henry Crerar, closed on Falaise. Although the movement to trap the Germans in the Falaise Pocket was excruciatingly slow at times, and many Germans escaped to fight another day, 50,000 were killed or captured in the encirclement and much of the Germans'

US Sherman tanks come ashore at Anzio during Operation Shingle in Italy. (US Army via Wikimedia Commons)

heavy weapons and equipment was lost. It was a crippling blow for the defenders.

On August 25, the city of Paris was liberated. Great celebrations took place in the streets of the French capital, and General Charles de Gaulle, a national hero, assumed governmental authority. General Dietrich von Choltitz, commander of the German garrison in the city, had chosen not to follow orders when Hitler demanded the destruction of the City of Light. Instead, Choltitz opted to preserve the cultural and artistic treasures of Paris and surrendered to the French 2nd Armoured Division.

By May, Soviet forces had pressed into the Crimea and taken the fortress city of Sevastopol after bottling up thousands of German troops in the south and rendering them inert in a vast 'prison camp'. As 1944 has become known as the year of Soviet Premier Josef Stalin's 'Ten Blows', the vengeful Red Army was on the move with Operation Bagration.

One of the largest and most successful offensive operations of World War Two, Bagration was launched two weeks after the Western Allied landings in Normandy. Its objectives were to eject the Germans from Belorussia and push into the Baltic States and eastern Poland while isolating German Army Group North and preventing the Germans from transferring reinforcements to France. Operation Bagration was quite successful as the Red Army covered vast areas of territory that had been under German occupation since 1941.

General Mark Clark inspects a unit of the US 34th Infantry Division after the liberation of Rome. (Brazilian National Archives via Wikimedia Commons)

However, when Soviet spearheads reached the outskirts of Warsaw, the Polish capital, Stalin callously ordered his forces to halt while the Home Army had risen inside the city to fight the Nazis. The Soviets allowed the Nazis to brutally suppress the Warsaw uprising simply because Stalin considered the Home Army and its democratic supporters to be the most tangible opponents of the installation of a communist government in post-war Poland. Only after the Home Army had suffered tremendous casualties did the Soviets even offer humanitarian aid. When the Red Army did move to occupy Warsaw later, Moscow's domination of the Polish government was a fait accompli.

On the Italian front, the Allied Fifth and Eighth Armies slugged their way through the rugged, mountainous country that was ideal for the defenders. German Field Marshal Albert Kesselring conducted a masterful defensive campaign, but in the end Allied power prevailed. In January, the Allied VI Corps had landed at Anzio in an abortive attempt to flank the Gustav Line, and it was not until May when General Harold Alexander, commander of the Allied 15th Army Group, unleashed Operation Diadem that the formidable defences were breached at Cassino, the linkup with the forces fighting their way out of the Anzio beachhead was accomplished, and the general advance northward was energised.

General Mark Clark, commanding Fifth Army, was enamoured with capturing Rome, the Eternal City. Although Alexander had indicated that the priority was to move to cut off the retreating Germans, Clark diverted forces to take Rome, delivering the glittering prize into his hands but at least somewhat forfeiting the opportunity to trap thousands of enemy troops. Clark's moment of glory was fleeting. After he rode into Rome in triumph on June 4, the D-Day landings swept the capture of the Eternal City from the newspaper headlines and the Italian campaign became a footnote to the war in France.

The war in the Pacific was characterised by the eclipse of Japanese naval air power at the Battle of the Philippine Sea in June 1944. The US Fifth Fleet under Admiral Raymond A. Spruance inflicted a devastating defeat on the Imperial Japanese Navy, its fighter pilots shooting down so many rising sun-emblazoned planes that the encounter was nicknamed the 'Great Marianas Turkey Shoot'. The Japanese also lost three aircraft carriers and more than 600 planes during the debacle.

While the US Navy was scoring big offshore, the Marines and US Army troops assaulted the Marianas, capturing the islands of Saipan, Guam, and Tinian and bringing the Japanese home islands within range of big American Boeing B-29 Superfortress bombers that would – in just a few months – lay waste to the major cities of Japan.

In the midst of stunning Allied victories, there was little time to assess the human impact of the costliest war in human history. Of course, there was an awareness of the casualties, the many dead and wounded, and the destruction wrought. But another cruel dimension was just becoming evident – the depth of Nazi depravity in the Holocaust.

Pictured in 1940, Anne Frank perished in a Nazi concentration camp but left a diary that moved the world. (European Union via Wikimedia Commons)

US Marines fire a 75mm howitzer against Japanese positions on the island of Saipan in the Marianas. (US Marine Corps via Wikimedia Commons)

On August 4, one of the most poignant and tragic events of the war took a decided turn. The Frank family, including teenage daughter Anne, and other Jewish citizens of Amsterdam were arrested by the Gestapo and taken to concentration camps after hiding in their 'secret annex' for months. Anne and her sister Margot died in the Bergen-Belsen camp in early 1945.

Anne's father, Otto Frank, survived the war and was instrumental in the publication of the young girl's diary, a primary document describing life in the shadow of Nazi persecution. *The Diary of a Young Girl* remains today one of the best-known books on the Holocaust. A stark reminder of man's inhumanity to man, the diary is not only part of the historical record, but also a warning to future generations that are confronted with the prospect of tyranny.

A Japanese bomb narrowly misses the aircraft carrier USS *Bunker Hill* during the Battle of the Philippine Sea. (US Navy via Wikimedia Commons)

ANTWERP LIBERATED

On September 4, 1944, the British 11th Armoured Division rumbled into the city of Antwerp, Belgium, the second largest port in Europe. Belgian Resistance fighters had already taken control of numerous key objectives within the city, and the speed of the movement by the British forces had sent the Germans packing so swiftly that they have been unable to destroy or disable Antwerp's port facilities that stretch for 26 miles along its waterfront.

Following the breakout from the Normandy beachhead, Allied forces surged forward during the summer of 1944. Advancing to the north and east, however, their supply lines lengthened appreciably, depleting reserves of petrol, food, and ammunition rapidly. Although the deepwater French port of Cherbourg, 350 miles from the frontlines in early September, was in Allied hands, the Nazis had made a shambles of its heavy equipment and facilities for offloading ships before their surrender. Meanwhile, the enemy stubbornly defended the English Channel ports of Boulogne, Dunkirk, and Calais after Hitler declared each of them 'fortress cities'.

Weeks after the Normandy landings, the primary avenue of Allied supply remained the D-Day beaches themselves, particularly the artificial Mulberry harbour at Arromanches. Due to the sheer volume of supplies required, the situation was unsustainable for a lengthy ground campaign. Therefore, the opening of Antwerp to Allied shipping was a priority among senior Allied commanders, topping everyone's list except that of General Bernard Montgomery, commander of the 21st Army Group. Montgomery was fixated with the prospect of a combined airborne/ground offensive, later dubbed Operation Market Garden, that would strike more than 60 miles into the Netherlands, across major rivers, and rapidly into the Ruhr, the industrial heart of Germany. If Market Garden succeeded, Montgomery asserted that World War Two in Europe would be over by Christmas 1944.

The issue with Antwerp was its location, 60 miles inland from the North Sea at the head of the estuary of the River Scheldt. Liberating Antwerp was one thing; opening the port to Allied shipping was quite another. The Germans – in substantial strength – held the approaches to the great port, the river banks, the small islands, and the ribbons of waterways that coursed toward the open sea. They had to be rooted out, and while Montgomery allocated the bulk of his forces to the upcoming Market Garden effort, he detailed the First Canadian Army the task of clearing the Scheldt estuary.

German prisoners are marched through the streets of Antwerp after British troops liberate the city. (Collections of the Imperial War Museums)

Above: Citizens of Antwerp gather around a British crew and its 17-pounder anti-tank gun in Antwerp. (Collections of the Imperial War Museums)

Left: Trucks are offloaded from an Allied freighter on the docks at Antwerp after the opening of the port. (US Army via Wikimedia Commons)

As the Canadian forces, under General Guy Simonds, were preparing for the monumental task before them, which included some of the toughest fighting of the war, Operation Market Garden failed in mid-September. Undertaken in early October, the effort to clear the Scheldt estuary took roughly five weeks and resulted in more than 6,300 Canadian casualties. The Germans had eventually denied the Allies use of Antwerp for 85 critical days.

DOLLE DINSDAG

On Dolle Dinsdag, or 'Mad Tuesday', masses of German soldiers, members of the Dutch Nazi Party, and pro-Nazi sympathizers literally ran for their lives. An estimated 65,000 troops and civilians clamoured to move out of the southern Netherlands, many of them headed for the border with neighbouring Germany, after radio announcements indicated that the liberation of the country by Allied troops is at hand.

The day after British forces occupied Antwerp, Belgium, radio broadcasts suggested that the Allies had advanced into The Netherlands and taken the Dutch city of Breda, 36 miles to the northeast. One of the radio broadcasts that started the rumour was made by Pieter Gerbrandy, the exiled Dutch Prime Minister, and thousands of Dutch civilians listened on Radio Oranje. At least two such announcements were made, and spontaneous celebrations broke out in the streets of many Dutch cities.

While crowds teemed in the towns, dancing and waving Allied and Dutch national flags, many German or pro-Nazi officials fled The Netherlands. Documents were destroyed, code books were burned, and belongings were packed as it appeared that the arrival of the Allied forces in the south of the country was imminent. Adding to the speculation, underground newspapers printed banner headlines that proclaimed the impending day of liberation.

Arthur Seyss-Inquart, Nazi Reich Commissioner for the Occupied Netherlands, fuelled speculation even further with a radio announcement of his own that declared a state of siege in the country. "The population must maintain order," he declared. "It is strictly forbidden to flee areas that are threatened by the enemy…any resistance to the occupation forces will be suppressed with force of weaponry…."

In reality, Allied troops did not liberate Breda until the end of October. However, British Field Marshal Bernard Montgomery's Operation Market Garden, an airborne/ground offensive conceived to reach the Ruhr, Germany's industrial centre, and end World War Two in Europe by Christmas 1944, was launched on September 17. In support of this military effort, the Dutch government-in-exile in London called for a railway strike to immobilise German troop transport in response to Market Garden; 30,000 workers heeded the direction.

Above: Dutch girls dance in the street in the city of Rotterdam on Dolle Dinsdag. (European Union via Wikimedia Commons)

Right: Arthur Seyss-Inquart was the Third Reich commissioner in The Netherlands on Dolle Dinsdag. (European Union via Wikimedia Commons)

Operation Market Garden failed within a week, but Allied forces did gain control of some Dutch territory. Still, the concerted offensive to liberate The Netherlands was not undertaken until the spring of 1945. The railroad strike carried on until that time and contributed to Nazi reprisals, including cutting off of food and fuel supplies through the winter of 1944, precipitating the 'Hunger Winter' in which an estimated 22,000 Dutch civilians died of starvation, disease, or exposure.

Queen Wilhelmina of The Netherlands delivers an address on Radio Oranje, a Dutch programme broadcast on the BBC. (European Union via Wikimedia Commons)

FIRST V-2 ROCKET ATTACKS

On September 8, 1944 civilians first became aware of Germany's technological advances in long range terror with the first launches of V-2 rockets. Two struck London and one hit Paris. A woman was killed in the blast when one of the rockets exploded in the Chiswick area of London.

Along with the V-1 flying bomb, the V-2, the world's first operational ballistic missile, was foremost among the so-called 'Vengeance Weapons' that Adolf Hitler unveiled in World War Two with the delusional belief that their employment would alter the outcome of the conflict in Europe. Nazi Propaganda Minister Josef Goebbels once stated publicly of the V-2: "I am told by the Führer that the big rocket bomb weighs 14 tons. This of course is a devastating murder weapon. I suspect that when the first projectiles plunge down into London, the English public will panic."

This bold prediction, of course, did not happen.

The V-1 flying bomb, forerunner of the modern cruise missile and often referred to as the 'Buzz Bomb' or 'Doodle Bug', was powered by a pulse jet engine and carried an 1,830lb warhead with a range of 149 miles. From launch sites in Nazi-occupied Europe, the V-1s were directed toward Allied cities and other targets. When the V-1 ran out of fuel, it plummeted randomly earthward, often detonating in civilian areas. From 1944, nearly 10,000 V-1s were launched against Britain and 2,500 against the Belgian port city of Antwerp after its liberation. Nearly 23,000 people were killed or wounded as a result of Buzz Bomb attacks.

The V-2 rocket was the ancestor of modern intercontinental ballistic missiles, now capable of carrying nuclear warheads, as well as tactical short-range missiles. Powered by a propellant mixture of ethanol and liquid oxygen, the V-2's rocket engine produced 56,000lb of thrust and carried the missile and its 2,205lb warhead to an altitude of approximately 50 miles, and like the V-1, when the fuel supply was consumed the V-2 plunged in freefall to the ground.

During the course of World War Two, more than 3,000 V-2 rockets were launched from various sites under Nazi control. London, Paris,

German soldiers move a V1 Buzz Bomb into position for launching. (Bundesarchiv Bild via Wikimedia Commons)

This RAF reconnaissance photo shows some of the research facility at Peenemunde where the V2 rocket was developed. (United Kingdom Government via Wikimedia Commons)

The damaged tail section of a V2 rocket is viewed by citizens of Antwerp after its capture.
(Jan B.H.A. Vervloedt (photo) Ad Meskens (scan) via Wikimedia Commons)

Wernher von Braun stands with German Army officers at the Peenemunde research facility.
(Bundesarchiv Bild via Wikimedia Commons)

Liege, Brussels, Antwerp, and locations in Luxembourg were among its targets, and more than 7,500 casualties, many of them civilians, resulted. The Germans designated their ballistic missile the A-4 and worked to develop a longer-range version, the A-9, featuring stabilising wings that contributed to extended range. The A-10 booster was intended to increase the V-2's range to thousands of miles and perhaps provide the capacity to strike the United States. The range of the standard V-2 was approximately 205 miles, capable of reaching major cities in Britain. The V-2 was mobile, transported on a meillerwagen trailer, and required only about an hour of preparation to launch. The missile was 46ft long and weighed 2,800lb. In flight the V-2 reached an astonishing top speed of 3,580mph.

As the war in Europe progressed, the capture of the V-1 and V-2 launch sites became a priority for Allied ground forces, and indeed there was an element of terror in the use of these weapons, much of which lay in the sheer randomness of their impact. British Prime Minister Winston Churchill declared: "The employment of this weapon represents a new effort by the enemy to shake the morale of our civilian population. In doing so, they have false hopes of preventing the threatened defeat on the field by that means."

Although defiant and confident that the British people and others affected by the terror weapons would buck up and remain steadfast until victory was won, Churchill nevertheless wanted the V-1 and V-2 threats removed as soon as possible. The weapons were developed by a cadre of brilliant German scientists and engineers at Peenemunde, a research facility on the island of Usedom in the Baltic Sea just off the coast of Germany. The weapons were built primarily by slave labour supplied from concentration camps. The labourers were kept in deplorable conditions and simply worked to death in many cases. Aerial reconnaissance photos revealed the existence of the facilities at Peenemunde and of the terror weapons in development as early as 1943. Royal Air Force and US Army Air Forces bombing raids were stepped up to impede the progress of the

German research, and in response some of the facilities were moved underground or into caves.

During the waning days of the war, the Western Allies conducted Operation Paperclip, an effort to bring German technology to the West for evaluation. Along with many components of the V-1 and V-2 that were recovered and shipped to the United States, numerous German scientists who had worked on the projects also came to America. Foremost among them was Dr Wernher von Braun, who continued his work with the US military and as a pioneer in the US space programme.

Among other responsibilities, von Braun served as director of the Marshall Space Flight Center in Huntsville, Alabama and as the chief architect of the Saturn V rocket booster that propelled the NASA (National Aeronautics and Space Administration) Apollo programme to the moon.

Left: While serving as director of the Marshall Space Flight Center in Huntsville, Alabama, Dr Wernher von Braun posed for this portrait in 1960.
(NASA/Marshall Space Flight Center via Wikimedia Commons)

Right: A V2 rocket stands on display at the research facility at Peenemunde.
(AElfwine via Wikimedia Commons)

SECOND QUEBEC CONFERENCE BEGINS

Although concerns regarding the tactical military situation in the China-Burma-India theatre continued, Allied forces were gaining the upper hand on all areas of combat operations. President Franklin D. Roosevelt and Prime Minister Winston Churchill met for the second time in the city of Quebec. Canadian Prime Minister William Mackenzie King hosted the meeting, which also included representatives of the Combined Chiefs of Staff and other high-level advisors, but which did not directly participate in the meetings. Soviet Premier Josef Stalin was invited to attend but declined due to the pressing nature of unfolding events on the Eastern Front.

Code named Octagon, the conference was convened to further discussions surrounding the anticipated postwar Allied occupation zones in Germany, and the controversial Morgenthau Plan, authored principally Henry Morgenthau, which sought a punitive peace with the German nation. Morgenthau, US treasury secretary and a close advisor to FDR, sought to strip Germany of its capacity to make war in the future, which meant the confiscation or destruction of heavy industry, manufacturing capabilities, and the reorientation of the people to a more agrarian economy.

Initially, Roosevelt and Churchill supported the Morgenthau plan, but considerable opposition was later encountered. US Secretary of War Henry L. Stimson opposed the plan on humanitarian grounds, fearing widespread famine and economic calamity that would further burden postwar Europe. Despite such discourse, on May 10, 1945, President Harry Truman authorised Occupation Directive 1067, which specified that US occupation troops would "take no steps looking toward the economic rehabilitation of Germany." Two years later, however, more pragmatic influences led to the adoption of JCS 1779, which noted, "An orderly, prosperous Europe requires the economic contributions of a stable and productive Germany."

Other topics discussed during the five days of the 1944 Quebec Conference included the continuation of the tremendously successful Lend Lease programme of military and economic aid

President Franklin D. Roosevelt and Prime Minister Winston Churchill confer during the Second Quebec Conference. (US National Archives and Records Administration via Wikimedia Commons)

from the United States to Great Britain and other countries, and the current state of the effort to produce a nuclear bomb along with the protocol for its use against Imperial Japan while preventing such arms from being possessed by the Soviet Union if possible.

Another interesting discussion surrounded the potential contribution of the British Royal Navy to the war in the Pacific. When Churchill extended the offer to send British warships to the area, Roosevelt enthusiastically agreed, to the chagrin of some senior US naval officers. However, in the capable hands of Admiral Bruce Fraser, the Royal Navy in the Pacific cooperated fully with the Americans. Fraser is remembered today as perhaps the most popular of high-ranking British officers in terms of relations with his American allies.

Left: Dignitaries gather during Prime Minister William Mackenzie King's reception at the Second Quebec Conference. (Library and Archives Canada via Wikimedia Commons)

Below: US Treasury Secretary Henry Morgenthau presented a controversial plan for postwar Germany that was discussed at Quebec. (Yousuf Karsh Netherlands Government via Wikimedia Commons)

US FORCES LAND ON PELELIU

On September 15, American troops of the III Amphibious Corps splashed ashore on the island of Peleliu in the Palaus group approximately 600 miles east of the Philippines. While the veteran 1st Marine Division assaulted Peleliu, a speck of land encompassing just five sq miles, elements of the US Army's 81st Infantry Division landed on nearby Angaur, six miles to the southwest.

The fight for Peleliu was one of the bloodiest of World War Two in the Pacific, and controversy surrounds Operation Stalemate II to this day. General Douglas MacArthur, commanding Allied forces in the South West Pacific Area, advocated the capture of the island and its airfield to secure the right flank of his pending invasion of the Philippines and eliminate the risk of Japanese air attacks against his troop transport and supply lines. But Admiral William F. 'Bull' Halsey, commanding the US Navy's Third Fleet, believed the operation to be unnecessary and proposed that it be cancelled.

Admiral Chester W. Nimitz, commander-in-chief of Pacific Ocean areas, sided with MacArthur and ordered Operation Stalemate II to proceed, although he did support Halsey's suggestion that that actual invasion of the Philippines should be moved up from December to October 1944 and redirected to the central island of Leyte rather than the island of Mindanao to the south.

As the 1st Marine Division prepared to assault Peleliu, its commander, Marine General William Rupertus, was confident that the operation would be swift. "Rough but fast…We'll be through in three days. It might only take two," he boasted. In the event, the roughly 10,000 Japanese defenders were waiting and unleashed a torrent of

Above: A medic gives a wounded US Marine water during the bitter fighting on Peleliu. (US Department of Defense via Wikimedia Commons)

RIght: General William Rupertus, commander of the 1st Marine Division, seriously underestimated the fight that lay ahead for control of Peleliu. (US Marine Corps via Wikimedia Commons)

small-arms, mortar, and artillery fire on the crowded beaches. After 74 days of fighting, pockets of Japanese resistance still held out, but Peleliu was declared secure. After taking Angaur, the 81st Division had come to the assistance of the Marines on the island, even though Rupertus wanted to keep the intense battle for Peleliu a 'Marines only' affair.

The fighting on Peleliu was so intense due to the failure of American reconnaissance flights and photo analysts to accurately gauge the rugged terrain, its deep draws, cliffs, and caves that provided cover and concealment for the defenders. Another factor was a change in enemy defensive strategy. While still contesting the beaches, the Japanese opted for a defence in depth to bleed the Americans white and exact a heavy price, one that might make the US tire of war and seek peace terms as casualties climbed amid continuing amphibious operations.

When the battle for Peleliu was over, the 1st Marine Division had been devastated with 1,300 dead, 5,450 wounded, and 36 missing in the deep jungle. The 81st Infantry Division lost 3,000 casualties on Angaur and Peleliu, including 468 killed in action. The Japanese garrison was virtually annihilated.

Under heavy Japanese fire, US Marines struggle forward on the island of Peleliu in the Palaus. (US Department of Defense via Wikimedia Commons)

OPERATION MARKET GARDEN BEGINS

It was the operation intended to end the war by Christmas. British and American airborne forces descending from the sky across the countryside of the southern Netherlands while Allied ground forces advanced across the frontier from Belgium. Operation Market Garden was under way.

Conceived by Field Marshal Bernard Montgomery, commander of the Allied 21st Army Group, Market Garden involved the seizure of key bridges successively across the Maas, Waal, and Lower Rhine Rivers and other waterways of the southern Netherlands by the 101st and 82nd US Airborne Divisions and the British 1st Airborne Division. These airborne forces would then hold open a narrow highway corridor that stretched 63 miles to the town of Arnhem while the armoured spearheads of the British XXX Corps raced to relieve each airborne division in turn, finally reaching Arnhem and establishing a critical bridgehead across the Lower Rhine.

From there, Montgomery envisioned a dagger thrust into Nazi Germany, then seizing the Ruhr, industrial nexus of the Third Reich, and ending World War Two in Europe by Christmas 1944 as Hitler and the Nazis were deprived of the vast majority of their industrial

General Frederick 'Boy' Browning (left), commander of the I Airborne Corps, and General James Gavin, commander of the 82nd Airborne Division, confer in The Netherlands. (Regional Archives Nijmegen via Wikimedia Commons)

Shown in a famous photograph while campaigning in North Africa, Field Marshal Bernard Montgomery was the father of Operation Market Garden. (US Department of Defense via Wikimedia Commons)

A paratrooper of the 101st Airborne Division comes down awkwardly in a Dutch field as Operation Market Garden opens. (US Army via Wikimedia Commons)

capacity. Montgomery chose to prioritise Market Garden over the opening of the estuary of the River Scheldt and the deepwater port of Antwerp to relieve continuing Allied resupply problems.

While the Western Allies, led by supreme commander General Dwight D. Eisenhower, pursued a broad front strategy after the D-Day landings of June 1944 and the breakout from Normandy the following month, Market Garden was a departure from such a prosecution of the war. It was also out of character for its principal advocate. Montgomery was the master of the set piece battle, well known for his meticulous planning, and Market Garden was daring, fraught with risk, and put together hastily. General Omar Bradley, commanding the Allied 12th Army Group, was stunned when the plan was presented.

Although the airborne, or 'Market', phase of the offensive began favourably, the airdrops and glider landings occurring amid excellent weather conditions and with great accuracy, there were significant troubles ahead. The 101st Airborne Division was tasked with capturing the bridges at Son and Veghel, while liberating the town of Eindhoven to the south. The Germans blew up the Son bridge just as the paratroopers approached, and hours were required for the construction of a Bailey bridge for XXX Corps use. In the meantime, XXX Corps progress had been painfully slow as the tanks and armoured vehicles were harried by German defenders, knocked out tanks had to be cleared from the narrow roadway, and troops had to deploy to root out the stubborn enemy.

The 82nd Airborne Division was first concerned with securing high ground surrounding its landing zones for the subsequent arrival of

British Paras pick their way through ruins in Oosterbeek, a western suburb of Arnhem. (Collections of the Imperial War Museums via Wikimedia Commons)

British paratroopers captured by the Germans at Arnhem are marched into captivity. (Collections of the Imperial War Museums via Wikimedia Commons)

reinforcing troops and supplies. Therefore, the bridges across the Waal at Nijmegen remained in German hands for an extended period. The paratroopers fought pitched battles with the enemy in the streets and houses of Nijmegen, and the assistance of the XXX Corps vanguard was required to finally clear the town. The heroic river crossing of the Waal by the 3rd Battalion, 504th Parachute Infantry Regiment, supported by the tanks and infantry of the Irish Guards, finally took the road bridge.

The Red Devils of the 1st Airborne Division had drawn the toughest assignment in capturing the bridge over the Lower Rhine at Arnhem. Difficulties plagued the operation from the start. The closest suitable drop and glider landing zones were eight miles away from the objective, and radio communications were disrupted. General Roy Urquhart, commanding the 1st Airborne Division, was separated from his staff for hours while dodging German patrols.

The Red Devils fought their way toward Arnhem but encountered unexpectedly stiff enemy resistance. The bulk of the division was stopped short of the bridge. Only the 2nd Battalion, Parachute Regiment, under Lieutenant Colonel John Frost, reached the span. Frost's paras fought gallantly for several days against German counter-attacks intent on dislodging their hold on the north end of Arnhem bridge. Eventually, Frost's command was overwhelmed and its survivors surrendered. The 1st Airborne Division was shattered, its remnants evacuated after approximately 80% of its 10,000 fighting men had been killed, wounded or captured.

Although XXX Corps spearheads had crossed the Waal at Nijmegen, only about 11 miles from Arnhem, the British armour could not proceed without infantry support up the single road to the relief of the beleaguered 1st Airborne, and Operation Market Garden ended in failure. Further contributing to the outcome were adverse weather conditions that delayed airborne reinforcement and resupply, the narrow single-lane road that XXX Corps was obliged to follow, and the presence of the German II SS Panzer Korps in the vicinity of Arnhem, its two divisions, the 9th and 10th SS Panzer, refitting after action in Normandy with their tanks and armoured vehicles precisely positioned where the lightly-armed British airborne were to advance.

In the decades since Market Garden, much debate has swirled around the Allied dismissal of intelligence reports that indicated the presence of the two German SS armoured divisions near Arnhem. Further, the strength and swiftness of the general German response to the Allied thrust was a rude surprise for Allied senior officers who believed the Nazis were thoroughly beaten in the autumn of 1944. The German Army, as it turned out, was far from finished and still capable of putting up a tremendous fight. Despite the failure of Market Garden, Allied forces retained control of some hard-won territory in The Netherlands, which was used as a springboard for future operations.

Montgomery defended the Market Garden initiative, which General Frederick 'Boy' Browning, commander of the I Airborne Corps, had described as "a bridge too far."

In his 1958 memoir, Montgomery commented, "It was a bad mistake on my part – I underestimated the difficulties of opening up the approaches to Antwerp…I reckoned the Canadian Army could do it while we were going for the Ruhr. I was wrong… In my – prejudiced – view, if the operation had been properly backed from its inception, and given the aircraft, ground forces, and administrative resources necessary for the job, it would have succeeded in spite of my mistakes, or the adverse weather, or the presence of the 2nd SS Panzer Corps in the Arnhem area. I remain Market Garden's unrepentant advocate."

Sherman tanks of the Irish Guards, XXX Corps are shown on the road to Arnhem during Operation Market Garden. (Collections of the Imperial War Museums via Wikimedia Commons)

An American field headquarters is located in the village of Hürtgen during the bitter fighting.
(US Government via Wikimedia Commons)

A German artillery piece fires at American positions during the Battle of the Hürtgen Forest.
(Bundesarchiv Bild via Wikimedia Commons)

BATTLE OF THE HÜRTGEN FOREST UNDERWAY

By the autumn of 1944 the Allies had pushed from Normandy to the German frontier and the fortifications of the Siegfried Line, or West Wall. It was the longest battle in the history of the US Army and the intensity didn't let up.

The Allies were eager to breach the Siegfried Line, secure bridgeheads across the great River Rhine, and penetrate deep into Germany. With the objective of occupying the Ruhr, the centre of German industry. The US First Army, under General Courtney Hodges was already engaged in heavy fighting at Aachen, the ancient city of Charlemagne and the Holy Roman Empire. The city would become the first major population centre in Germany to fall to the Western Allies in October.

In the meantime, Hodges and his subordinate General J. Lawton Collins, commanding the VII Corps, elected to continue the US advance to the south and east of Aachen through a densely wooded area of roughly 50 sq miles known as the Hürtgen Forest. The Hürtgen was no place to execute rapid military movement. Its terrain was often steep and rutted. There were few roads, and the thick forest negated the American advantages of air superiority and armour support that had been crucial in the advance from Normandy to this point.

Hodges and Collins discounted the option of bypassing the Hürtgen and decided to clear the enemy forces from it in order to protect the flank of the VII Corps advance toward the Rhine. Although the American generals made no immediate effort to secure them, seven dams along the course of the Roer River and its tributaries were critical for flood control of the surrounding valley. Soon enough the capture of the dams to prevent the Germans from flooding an area of future Allied advance became another priority for the Americans fighting in the Hürtgen Forest.

Although the Germans had not considered an American thrust into the forest likely, they had nevertheless fortified the area with bunkers, pillboxes, machine-gun nests, and minefields while committing elements of the Seventh, Fifteenth, and Fifth Panzer Armies to its defence. Early in their advance, the US ground troops ran into stiff opposition, and the fighting devolved into a bloody battle of attrition.

Not only did the American forces have to contend with stubborn veteran enemy troops, but also with the numbing cold, snow, sleet, and mud that characterised winter combat. Shortages of food, ammunition, and even replacements for the casualties sustained added to the misery. Famed author and war correspondent Ernest Hemingway conjured up images of a horrific campaign during the Great War a generation earlier when he described the fighting in the Hürtgen as "Passchendaele with tree bursts."

Historians have debated the perhaps ill-advised venture into the Hürtgen, considering that the early objective was only to cover the VII Corps flank amid the absence of any recognition of the importance of the dams that could prevent or isolate any significant movement across the Roer. An advance to the southeast would have avoided the forest entanglement, facilitated the rapid seizure of the dams, and then allowed the Americans to clear the surrounding area. In the event, however, the Germans were able to exact a heavy toll on the attackers, blunt their drive, and buy precious time while fighting from well-prepared defensive

An American halftrack negotiates a muddy road amid the difficult terrain of the Hürtgen Forest.
(US Army via Wikimedia Commons)

American soldiers move through the shattered village of Hürtgen in the autumn of 1944.
(US Army Signal Corps via Wikimedia Commons)

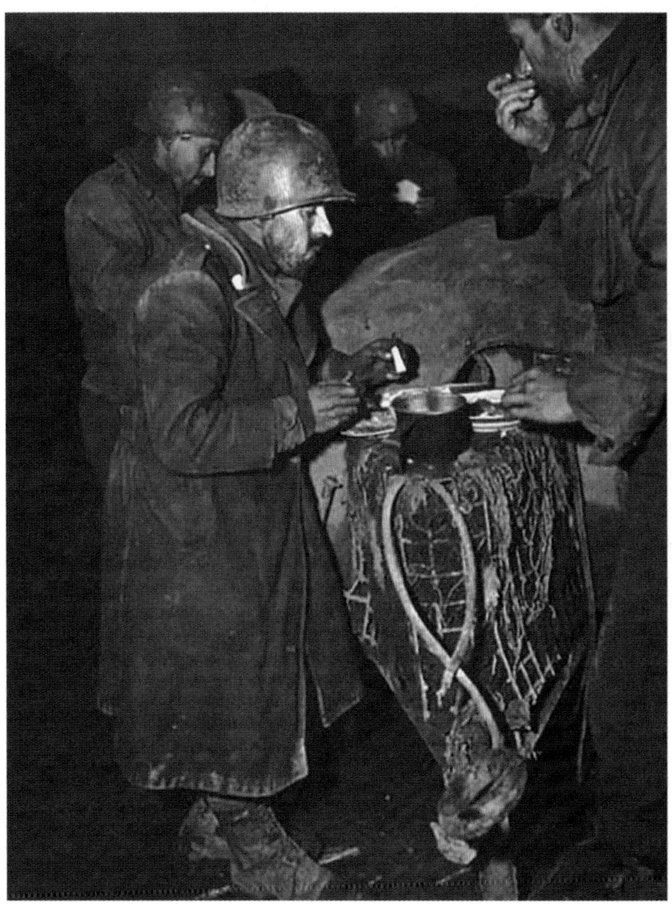

After days on the front line in the Hürtgen Forest an American soldier finally receives a hot meal.
(US Department of Defense via Wikimedia Commons)

positions. As the combat in the forest continued, the Americans fed more and more forces into the growing debacle. By the end of the battle, six infantry divisions, including the 9th, 28th, 8th, 1st, 78th, and 83rd had been at least partially committed piecemeal to the meatgrinder along with the 3rd and 5th Armored Divisions, the 517th Parachute Infantry Regiment, and the 2nd Ranger Battalion.

Nowhere else during World War Two was the mettle of the US infantryman tested more thoroughly. Hot food was non-existent, trench foot was rampant, winter clothing became caked with mud and ice and too heavy to wear. One soldier recalled, "The forest up there was a hell of an eerie place to fight. Show me a man who went through the battle and who says he never had a feeling of fear, and I'll show you a liar. You can't get all of the dead because you can't find them, and they stay there to remind the guys advancing as to what might hit them."

The terrible campaign in the Hürtgen dragged on until the Americans were ordered to withdraw in mid-December with the onset of the German Ardennes Offensive and the Battle of the Bulge.

The butcher's bill in the Hürtgen Forest was appalling. While approximately 120,000 US troops were engaged in the battle, 33,000 men were killed, wounded, captured, or withdrawn due to non-combat related circumstances. Some were suffering from illness or frostbite, while others had simply lost their composure after seemingly endless days on the frontline. One American officer forlornly assessed, "One way or another, they got you. You froze to death, or you got sick, or you got blown to bits." German casualties were estimated at 28,000.

Medics treat a wounded American soldier in a heavily wooded area of the Hürtgen Forest. (US Army Signal Corps via Wikimedia Commons)

MOSCOW CONFERENCE BEGINS

On October 9, 1944, British Prime Minister Winston Churchill and Soviet Premier Josef Stalin sat down to begin 10 days of discussions concerning the entry of the Soviet Union in the war against Japan and the shape of the postwar world, including proposed spheres of influence for the respective Allied powers in Europe following the defeat of the Third Reich. The meetings were held in the Soviet capital, and this fourth Moscow Conference was code named 'Tolstoy'.

Included in the discussions and as observers were British Foreign Minister Anthony Eden and Field Marshal Alan Brooke, chief of the Imperial General Staff, Soviet Foreign Minister Vyacheslav Molotov, US Ambassador to the Soviet Union Averill Harriman, and General John Dean, chief of the US military mission in Moscow.

Although there had been earlier discussions regarding Soviet participation in the Pacific War, from the beginning the Soviet leader seemed preoccupied with the distribution of relative influence across Europe after the defeat of the Nazis, particularly in the Balkans.

In his 1958 memoir, Churchill described a meeting with Stalin during which he produced a piece of paper and scribbled the names of countries and the percentages of Soviet and Western influence he envisioned during the years after World War Two. Among the nations included were Greece, Romania, Hungary, and Yugoslavia. The future of Poland was also discussed, although a proposed meeting between representatives of the Soviet government and the Polish government-in-exile was never held.

Prime Minister Winston Churchill greets a crowd in Quebec. He later met with Josef Stalin in Moscow to discuss spheres of influence. (National Archives and Records Administration via Wikimedia Commons)

Churchill recalled Stalin's review of the proposed levels of respective influence and the Soviet leader placing a large check mark in blue pencil at the top. Among these 'spheres' were a 90% Soviet influence in Romania, 75% in Bulgaria, and 50% in Yugoslavia and Hungary, while Britain would exert 90% influence in Greece with the acquiescence of the United States. Although President Franklin D. Roosevelt was said to have generally agreed with the arrangement, he was apparently perturbed with the allocation regarding Bulgaria.

According to one source, Churchill handed his preliminary proposal to Stalin, who considered it a moment before approving. Owing to its sensitivity, Churchill then suggested that the paper should be burned. However, Stalin urged that it should be retained, and it has generally been referred to since then as the 'Percentages Agreement'. The Prime Minister later called the paper a 'naughty document'. Reportedly, the percentages were points of discussion between Eden and Molotov as well during the meetings.

Some historians point to the supposed agreement as evidence of latent imperialism and the burgeoning Cold War since the leaders apparently brushed aside any real concern regarding the will of the peoples that had recently been or were in the process of being liberated.

Left: The Percentages Agreement as written by Churchill and endorsed by Stalin. (United Kingdom Government via Wikimedia Commons)

Right: Soviet Premier Josef Stalin worked to extend his influence across Eastern Europe during the fourth Moscow Conference. (Franklin D. Roosevelt Library via Wikimedia Commons)

FIELD MARSHAL ROMMEL COMMITS SUICIDE

After he had been implicated in the July 20, 1944, attempt to assassinate Hitler at his Wolf's Lair headquarters in East Prussia, Field Marshal Erwin Rommel chose to commit suicide by ingesting cyanide rather than face a show trial, public conviction, and execution as a traitor to the Führer and the Nazi regime to which he had pledged personal loyalty.

A national hero in Germany, Rommel was a career soldier, decorated for bravery in combat during World War One, and once commander of Hitler's personal bodyguard. After the outbreak of World War Two, Rommel commanded the 7th Panzer Division during the 1940 campaign in France, demonstrating his competence in the use of armour and skill as a military tactician.

Considered a favourite of Hitler, Rommel advanced rapidly in the higher ranks of the German Army and gained lasting fame as the commander of the vaunted Afrika Korps. He earned the nickname of the 'Desert Fox' while leading his command to dazzling victories against Allied forces in North Africa despite constantly facing shortages of supplies, weapons, and manpower. Rommel was ordered to return to Germany prior to the final Axis surrender in North Africa and placed in command of Army Group B in Normandy, responsible for defending the Atlantic Wall fortifications against an expected Allied invasion, which came on June 6, 1944, while he was at home in the town of Ulm, celebrating the birthday of his wife, Lucie. On July 17, after visiting the headquarters of the I SS Panzer Korps in Normandy, Rommel's staff car was strafed by an Allied fighter plane, and he was seriously wounded.

As the plot to assassinate Hitler widened prior to the July 20 attempt, Rommel was approached by the conspirators and asked to actively join with them. While it appears that he was resigned to the fact that the war was lost, Rommel did not commit to direct involvement, although he did confront Hitler with stark language regarding the ongoing deterioration of the military situation.

Historians debate the actual depth of Rommel's involvement in and knowledge of the conspiracy. However, as he recovered from the near-fatal

Rommel stands beside Hitler during the 1939 campaign in Poland. (Bundesarchiv Bild via Wikimedia Commons)

Field Marshal Rommel (right) confers with his chief of staff, General Hans Speidel, who was involved in the plot to assassinate Hitler. (Bundesarchiv Bild via Wikimedia Commons)

skull fractures sustained in Normandy, Rommel's fate was sealed. In the midst of a delirium, one conspirator continually muttered his name, and a second revealed under torture that Rommel was involved.

Gestapo agents placed Rommel's residence under surveillance, and on this date two army generals from Berlin arrived at his home. They delivered Hitler's ultimatum of death by suicide and a state funeral with full honours or the humiliation of a public trial and repercussions for his family. Further public reports would attribute the hero's death to the wounds received in July, preventing a serious blow to national morale.

The field marshal explained the situation to his wife and son, got into a car with the generals, and took the cyanide a few minutes later. Rommel's funeral was conducted in Ulm, and he was interred close to the family home in Herrlingen. The Führer proclaimed a national day of mourning.

Field Marshal Rommel's funeral procession courses along a street in Ulm. After committing suicide, the national hero was interred in Herrlingen. (Bundesarchiv Bild via Wikimedia Commons)

SUBSCRIBE TODAY!

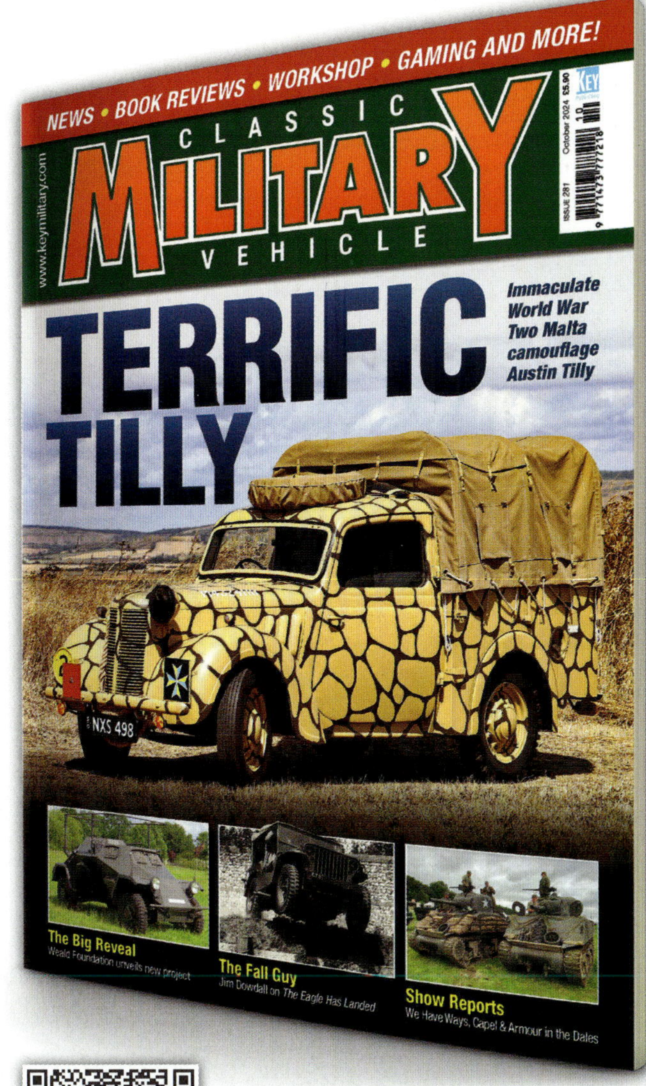

Britain at War - dedicated to exploring every aspect of the involvement of Britain and her Commonwealth in conflicts from the turn of the 20th century through to the present day.

Classic Military Vehicle is the best-selling publication in the UK dedicated to the coverage of all historic military vehicles.

from our online shop...
/collections/subscriptions

Free 2nd class P&P on all UK & BFPO orders. Overseas charges apply.

MacArthur Returns to the Philippines

Keeping a promise he had made when leaving the country following the Japanese invasion of early 1942, in company with President-in-Exile Sergio Osmena, General Douglas MacArthur, commander of Allied Forces in the Southwest Pacific, left a landing craft and waded ashore on the island of Leyte in the central Philippines. Two hours earlier, at around 10am, American soldiers of the US Sixth Army, under General Walter Kreuger, the first of 180,000 that would be committed to the liberation of the Philippines, had hit the beaches of Leyte, contrary to the Japanese belief that the Americans would land on the main island of Luzon well to the north.

Nearly three years earlier, MacArthur's American and Filipino forces had suffered a humiliating defeat at the hands of the Japanese, and the Philippines had been under the brutal heel of Japanese occupation since that time. President Franklin D. Roosevelt ordered MacArthur to evacuate to safety in Australia rather than be captured by the enemy, and when he arrived in Melbourne, the general had proclaimed, "I came through, and I shall return!"

MacArthur was given command of Allied forces in the region and since then had fought to honour his

US soldiers of the 12th Cavalry Regiment move inland from the beachhead on the Philippine island of Leyte. (US Army Signal Corps Archive via Wikimedia Commons)

General Douglas MacArthur wades ashore on the island of Leyte during his dramatic return to the Philippines. (US Army Signal Corps via Wikimedia Commons)

American artillerymen fire the 105mm howitzer aboard an M7 Priest self-propelled platform in Leyte. (US Government via Wikimedia Commons)

pledge. Leading an offensive through various island assaults and heavy combat along the northern shores of New Guinea, he had successfully persuaded President Roosevelt to proceed with the liberation of the Philippines rather than a more northerly approach to the island of Formosa, which had been advocated by senior naval officers.

Finally, MacArthur made good on his pledge, and after spending two hours observing the progress of the assault on Leyte, he stepped to a microphone and delivered a stirring address. "People of the Philippines, I have returned!" he roared. "Rally to me!...For your homes and hearths, strike! In the name of your sacred dead, strike!...Let no heart be faint. Let every arm be steeled…."

General Kreuger's troops made early gains toward the town of Tacloban, the capital of Leyte, and in securing the Leyte Valley, where airfields might be built. However, hopes for a swift victory were dashed as General Tomoyuki Yamashita, a veteran combat commander, reoriented his forces from Luzon to Leyte rapidly and mounted a concerted defence. At the same time, the US and Japanese navies were engaged in the epic Battle of Leyte Gulf, a resounding American victory but a close call, nonetheless.

Along with fighting the stubborn Japanese, whose strength grew eventually to about 65,000 troops on the island of Leyte, the Americans were obliged to contend with torrential rains that turned flatlands into muddy quagmires, as well difficult terrain that included dense, stifling jungle and imposing mountains and ridgelines. Fighting stretched into December before American forces captured the Japanese headquarters at Ormoc on the west coast of Leyte and the island was declared secure.

Although the Americans had taken Leyte and prepared for further landings in the Philippines, Japanese holdouts remained at large in the mountainous country of Leyte for many months.

LIBERATION OF BELGRADE

After nearly 1,300 days of Nazi occupation, on October 20, 1944, Soviet forces of the 3rd Ukrainian Front and the Liberation Army of Yugoslavia entered Belgrade, the capital of Yugoslavia. Soviet Premier Josef Stalin and Marshal Josip Broz Tito, leader of the partisan opposition to the Germans, had reached an understanding to cooperate with regard to the operation that liberates Belgrade.

Planning for the Belgrade Offensive had begun in September 1944 with several objectives in mind. Not only was the liberation of the city a priority, but also the ejection of German forces from Serbia, which would effectively sever communication and supply links to Axis forces further south in the Balkans and Greece. The Soviet Red Army committed the 3rd Ukrainian Front, under Marshal Fyodor Tolbukhin, to the main offensive alongside the Yugoslav I Army Corps. To the south, the Bulgarian Second Army and the Yugoslav XIII Army Corps advanced. In the north, the 2nd Ukrainian Front, led by Marshal Rodion Malinovsky, also moved forward.

Bulgaria had joined the Allied cause after a coup d'etat in September, which deposed the government of the Kingdom of Bulgaria and replaced it with the pro-Soviet Fatherland Front. Within days of establishing the new government, the Bulgarians declared war on the Axis.

While strong Red Army forces were concentrated on the border between Yugoslavia and Bulgaria, a heavy air bombardment preceded the ground offensive, which commenced on October 12 against German Army Group F, under the command of Field Marshal Maximilian von Weichs. Within two days, the Soviets had broken through German defensive positions just south of Belgrade and were fighting on the outskirts of the city. The Yugoslavs came up, and the two forces advanced along the north and south banks of the River Sava.

While the fighting continued, thousands of German troops were cut off southeast of Belgrade, and the Soviets diverted forces to reduce the pocket, necessitating a brief pause in the advance. Meanwhile, the retirement of German Army Group E, under Colonel General Alexander Löhr, from Greece was underway. The Germans were subjected to stepped up partisan activity during the withdrawal, and the attempt of the Yugoslav XIII Corps and Bulgarian Second Army to cut off the retreat route was partially successful. Army Group E retired through the mountainous country of Montenegro and Bosnia, unable to reinforce German units fighting in Hungary.

Citizens of Belgrade inspect a Soviet tank destroyed during the liberation of the capital of Yugoslavia. (Mesta stradanja i antifašističke borbe u Beogradu 1941–44 via Wikimedia Commons)

After eight days of combat, Belgrade was completely in Soviet and Yugoslav control. The success of the Belgrade Offensive, which was designated as one of Stalin's Ten Blows of 1944, facilitated further campaigning beyond the River Danube, and the stage was set for the upcoming offensive against Budapest, the capital of Axis Hungary.

Troops and tanks of the 3rd Ukrainian Front advance toward Belgrade in October 1944. (Russian Federation via Wikimedia Commons)

Yugoslav partisans march victoriously through the streets of Belgrade after the liberation of the city. (Zbornik sećanja aktivista jugoslovenskog revolucionarnog radničkog pokreta, knjiga šesta via Wikimedia Commons)

AACHEN FALLS

Aachen, the medieval city of the birth of Charlemagne and Hitler's focus as the centre of the 'First Reich', the Holy Roman Empire, a heritage that the Nazis claimed, fell to American troops after a difficult bout of urban combat. Aachen was the first major city in Germany itself to come under Allied control.

The rapid advance of two Allied army corps, the 12th under General Omar Bradley and the 21st under Field Marshal Bernard Montgomery, had brought Allied forces to the frontier of Nazi Germany by the late summer of 1944. The advance from Normandy had covered territory so swiftly against ebbing German resistance that the Allies were substantially ahead of schedule with leading elements holding ground in The Netherlands, Belgium, France, and Luxembourg.

Amid the rapid advance, the reduction of the Ruhr, the industrial heart of Germany, became a priority for the Allies, and for the American VII and XIX Corps, under Generals J. Lawton Collins and Charles H. Corlett, the road to the Ruhr was through Aachen. The two American corps, components of General Courtney Hodges' First Army, were tasked in September with taking the city and opening the 'Aachen Gap' to the Ruhr. Aachen and its environs offered a tough fight. The city had been incorporated into the formidable defences of the Siegfried Line, or West Wall, which guarded the German frontier. The prospect of street-to-street and house-to-house combat was daunting, and the strength of German fortifications along two defensive bands of the West Wall compounded the difficulty of the operation.

The battle for Aachen had begun on September 12, 1944, as elements of the US 1st Infantry Division penetrated enemy defences

Set up in an Aachen street, an American machine-gun crew fires on German positions in October 1944. (US Army via Wikimedia Commons)

The first US tank to enter Aachen pauses before turning along a city street during urban fighting. (US Department of Defense via Wikimedia Commons)

After their surrender in Aachen, German prisoners march out of the city and into captivity. (US Army via Wikimedia Commons)

south of the city. The primary opposition during more than five weeks of fighting that followed was to come from the 116th Panzer Division under General Gerhard Graf von Schwerin, which had suffered heavy losses in Normandy. The defenders numbered roughly 12,000, but only a handful of tanks and armoured vehicles had survived the Normandy defeat, and more than 5,000 Germans were killed, wounded, and captured in the battle for Aachen.

Although early gains fostered US optimism, German resistance quickly stiffened, and the Americans were obliged to beat back sporadic counterattacks. Supply shortages compelled Bradley to halt 12th Army Group operations temporarily. When the drive to take Aachen and move eastward resumed, American artillery pounded enemy positions, but progress was sluggish. In a single day, US heavy guns fired 5,000 shells in support of the infantry and armour committed to dislodge the enemy.

By October 19, the Americans had encircled the city, and the urban combat finally ended with the surrender of Aachen two days later. The route of advance to the Ruhr and the great River Rhine were open at a cost of 7,000 Americans killed or wounded.

BATTLE OF LEYTE GULF BEGINS

The four-day Battle of Leyte Gulf, the largest naval fight in military history, began across a wide expanse of the Pacific while ground forces had stormed ashore in the Philippines to begin the liberation of the islands from Japanese control.

By the autumn of 1944, the US and Allied push toward the Japanese home islands had advanced to the Philippines, tightening the noose of the two-pronged thrust in the south and central operations areas. American war planners saw success in the Philippines as a means of severing supply lines to enemy-occupied areas of the East Indies, providing bases as a springboard for further offensive operations toward Japan itself, and allowing US and Allied air, naval, and ground assets to reduce the combat efficiency of Japanese forces on the island of Formosa, coastal areas of China, and elsewhere on the mainland of Asia.

In response to the rising American threat, the high command of the Imperial Japanese Navy enacted Operation Sho-Go, a desperate attempt to stem the US tide by destroying the US supply and transport fleet supporting ground operations off the island of Leyte. True to form, Japanese admirals conceived a complex pincer movement with naval forces advancing on the Leyte area from two directions. Elsewhere, a decoy force would lure the big Essex class aircraft carriers and fast battleships of Admiral William F. 'Bull' Halsey's Third Fleet far to the north, where it would be chasing aircraft carriers whose decks were empty of aircraft since Japanese naval air strength had been decimated in earlier actions.

If successful, the decoy, or northern force, under Admiral Jisaburo Ozawa, would sacrifice itself so that the main battle forces, under the command of Admirals Takeo Kurita, Shoji Nishimura, and Kiyohide Shima could decimate the Leyte beachhead and shipping offshore. The vulnerable transports would be protected only by the small escort aircraft carriers, destroyers, and destroyer escorts of the US Seventh Fleet, under Admiral Thomas C. Kinkaid. These would be easily brushed aside. Sho-Go would at the very least buy precious time for the Japanese Empire.

While the decoy force moved north off Cape Engano, three Japanese task forces proceeded toward Leyte, Kurita and centre force via the Sibuyan Sea and San Bernardino Strait, Nishimura and Shima with two elements of southern force through the Mindanao Sea and Surigao Strait. If everything went according to plan, Kurita and his powerful force would become a "hawk among chickens," the southern forces adding to the havoc.

From the beginning, however, the Japanese plan became unwieldy. The US submarines *Darter* and *Dace* quickly sank the Japanese cruisers *Atago* and *Maya*. They had shadowed Kurita's force all day on October 23, alerting higher command that the Imperial Navy was at sea, and then pressed their successful attacks the next morning. Throughout the day on October 24, aircraft from six US carriers harassed Kurita, flying 259 sorties. They sank the behemoth super battleship *Musashi* with 17 bombs and 19 torpedoes. *Musashi*'s sister battleship *Yamato* was hit by three bombs and down by the bow, but *Yamato*'s 18in main batteries remained a formidable threat. Also on October 24, a lone Japanese bomber struck the US light carrier *Princeton* with

Right: The Japanese cruiser *Noshiro* manoeuvres violently to avoid US Navy aircraft at Leyte Gulf. (US Navy via Wikimedia Commons)

Below: The Japanese super battleship *Musashi* reels under heavy attack from US Navy planes during the Battle of Leyte Gulf. (US Navy via Wikimedia Commons)

The Japanese super battleship *Yamato* takes a direct hit from an American bomb in the Sibuyan Sea during the Battle of Leyte Gulf. (US Navy via Wikimedia Commons)

under Admiral Jesse Oldendorf, their primary role to provide shore bombardment and fire support for the troops on Leyte, diverted to block the passage of the Japanese. Oldendorf organised an ambush, and the Japanese, oblivious to their peril, sailed into the trap. The big guns of battleships *Tennessee*, *Maryland*, *California*, *Pennsylvania*, and *West Virginia*, all veterans that sustained heavy damage at Pearl Harbor in 1941, thundered in revenge along with those of the battleship *Mississippi*. The southern arm of the Japanese pincer was destroyed. Several Japanese battleships and cruisers were sunk. Only a single destroyer survived the engagement in Surigao Strait.

While Halsey sped recklessly toward Ozawa and the decoy force, the three escort carrier groups of 7th Fleet were all that stood between Kurita's centre force after the Japanese commander reversed course and headed once again for the Leyte invasion beaches. Designated

The 16in main batteries of the battleship USS *West Virginia* thunder against the hapless Japanese in Surigao Strait. (US Navy via Wikimedia Commons)

a single 550lb bomb, and the ensuing explosions doomed the ship while damaging the cruiser *Birmingham* that had come alongside to render aid.

Meanwhile, Halsey was aware of the decoy force and concerned that sufficient Japanese aircraft might remain to pose a threat to ongoing operations. Reports indicated that Kurita had withdrawn after suffering the earlier losses. Halsey concluded that Kurita was out of the fight, but his conclusion was premature. He set off in hot pursuit of Ozawa. Admiral Kinkaid was unaware that the fast battleships of Task Force 34 had joined in Halsey's race to the north.

As trouble brewed around the Leyte beachhead, the Japanese southern force came to grief at the Battle of Surigao Strait. Nishimura and Shima had been discovered, and Kinkaid ordered several old battleships

The aircraft carrier USS *Princeton* blazes after being hit by a Japanese bomb during the Battle of Leyte Gulf, October 24, 1944. (US Navy via Wikimedia Commons)

Far left: Admiral William F. 'Bull' Halsey chased the Japanese decoy force at the Battle of Leyte Gulf. (US Navy via Wikimedia Commons)

Left: Japanese Admiral Takeo Kurita may have snatched defeat from the jaws of victory during the Battle off Samar at Leyte Gulf. (Government of Japan via Wikimedia Commons)

the same, bluffing torpedo runs when their supply of the 'fish' was exhausted.

Although the American destroyers chased salvoes and took evasive action as they were able, the Japanese found the range eventually. *Johnston* and *Hoel* were sunk beneath a veritable rain of large-calibre enemy shells. *Samuel B. Roberts* also went down in a deluge of fire. The escort carrier *Gambier Bay* was sunk, while another, *Kitkun Bay*, took 15 hits but survived. Some of the heavy Japanese shells had passed right through the thin armour of the escort carriers without exploding. One other notable loss among the escort carriers was USS *St. Lo*, sunk by one of the first Kamikaze suicide plane attacks of the Pacific War.

Amid the uneven naval brawl that came to be known as the Battle off Samar, Kurita became convinced that he was facing Halsey's frontline battleships and aircraft carriers. Discretion got the better part of valour, and the Japanese admiral – on the brink of a decisive victory – broke off the engagement and ordered his force to retire back up San Bernardino Strait.

One American sailor with plenty of grit shouted, "Dammit boys! They're getting away"

During the ordeal of Taffy 3, Admiral Kinkaid repeatedly called for assistance, believing the battleships of Task Force 34 were still nearby. Admiral Chester Nimitz in Hawaii radioed a query: "WHERE IS RPT WHERE IS TASK FORCE 34 RR THE WORLD WONDERS?" When Halsey, otherwise engaged against the decoy force, received the message, he interpreted the last three words as a stinging rebuke from Nimitz. Actually, "THE WORLD WONDERS?" was mere padding meant to confuse any Japanese interceptors.

Halsey's aircraft did wreak havoc with Ozawa, sinking four Japanese aircraft carriers, one of them *Zuikaku*, the last survivor of the Pearl Harbor attack.

In the end, the Battle of Leyte Gulf was a near-run thing – and a resounding victory for the US Navy. The Japanese were no longer capable of a major naval offensive. Any future sorties were tantamount to suicide missions.

Admiral Halsey's conduct at Leyte Gulf remains a source of controversy to this day.

As the Japanese aircraft carrier *Zuikaku* lists heavily, crewmen salute their lowering flag before abandoning ship during the Battle of Leyte Gulf. (US Government captured enemy property via Wikimedia Commons)

Taffy 1, 2, and 3, the 'baby flattop' groups were primarily tasked with air support and anti-submarine patrol. However, those roles radically changed on the morning of October 25, when a Grumman TBF Avenger torpedo bomber relayed the ominous news that powerful Japanese warships were exiting San Bernardino Strait and bearing down on Leyte.

The northernmost of the escort carrier groups was Admiral Clifton A.F. Sprague's Taffy 3, and when he heard the news, he was taken aback. Sprague radioed for confirmation, and the pilot emphatically replied: "I can see pagoda masts, and I see the biggest meatball flag on the biggest battleship I ever saw." The time was shortly after 6:30am, and Taffy 3 was about to record one of the most stirring chapters in the history of the US Navy.

The small American ships had nothing heavier than a 5in gun among them. However, they sallied forth to launch repeated torpedo attacks against the big Japanese battleships and cruisers. The destroyers *Johnston, Heermann*, and *Hoel* hit as hard as they could, one torpedo blowing the bow off the Japanese cruiser *Kumano*. The swift destroyer escort *Samuel B. Roberts* fired more than 600 5in rounds, and at times the enemy ships were caught in the crossfire of multiple American 'pop guns'.

US Navy aircraft flew countless sorties, strafing with machine guns, dropping bombs meant for inshore targets, and even loosing depth charges at the Japanese warships. When they ran out of ordnance, the pilots made dummy attacks to draw fire. The little destroyers and destroyer escorts did

Shown in a postwar photo while entering the harbour at Monaco, the destroyer USS *Heermann* survived the desperate Battle off Samar during the Leyte Gulf fight. (US Navy via Wikimedia Commons)

OPERATION INFATUATE: CLEARING WALCHEREN ISLAND

The effort to clear the estuary of the River Scheldt and in turn the deepwater port of Antwerp, the second largest in Europe, continued with the assault on German-held Walcheren Island. Operation Infatuate completed the clearing of enemy troops from the estuary and finally opened Antwerp to Allied maritime traffic. At peak activity the port would handle 22,000 tons of supplies and equipment per day.

As Allied armies advanced across Europe from Normandy, supply lines were thinly stretched, and shortages of essential materiel sometimes ground offensive operations to a halt. The opening of the port of Antwerp became a priority for the Allies in the autumn of 1944. As Field Marshal Bernard Montgomery, leading 21st Army Group, was given the go-ahead for the ill-fated Operation Market Garden in The Netherlands by General Dwight Eisenhower, supreme commander of Allied forces in western Europe, Montgomery assigned the Canadian First Army, commanded by General Guy Simonds, to clear the Scheldt estuary.

British assault forces come ashore on Walcheren Island in the early morning of November 1, 1944. (Collections of the Imperial War Museums via Wikimedia Commons)

Royal Marine Commandos churn toward the shore of Walcheren Island aboard amphibious landing craft. (Collections of the Imperial War Museums via Wikimedia Commons)

Antwerp was situated 60 miles inland from the North Sea, and while the British 11th Armoured Division had rolled into the city on September 4, the Germans still controlled the estuary, the riverbanks, small islands, and waterways from the city to the sea, rendering the port facilities useless. They had also sown the river with mines.

When Operation Infatuate was launched, the Canadians had already been fighting for a month to clear the Scheldt. A three-step campaign was undertaken with Operation Switchback reducing German resistance in the Breskens Pocket in the south and Operation Vitality making rugged headway in the north and east. Some of the toughest fighting of World War Two had taken place, and these efforts were still underway when Operation Infatuate was set in motion to seize Walcheren Island, a spit of land 10 sq miles across and encompassing a total area of 83 sq miles.

Landings were slated for two points on the island, and various commando units were to lead the way with infantry and armoured formations to follow. According to intelligence reports, a formidable force of 7,000 to 10,000 Germans occupied strong defensive positions on Walcheren Island. After preliminary landings by Canadian troops to seize the narrow causeway between the mainland and Walcheren, a heavy naval bombardment touched off in support of the landings that began at 4:45am.

A week of hard fighting followed, and the last German resistance on Walcheren ceased on November 8, 1944. Allied casualties at Walcheren reached 1,500, while the five weeks of fighting necessary to clear the Scheldt estuary cost them 13,000 killed and wounded. German dead during the period totalled 12,000, and 41,000 were captured. Altogether, the enemy had denied the Allies use of Antwerp, which became operational on November 28, for 85 days.

Thousands of German prisoners rounded up on Walcheren Island await disposition in November 1944. (Collections of the Imperial War Museums via Wikimedia Commons)

FIELD MARSHAL SIR JOHN DILL DIES

A plastic Anaemia that had been diagnosed just the previous summer claimed the life of Field Marshal Sir John Dill, head of the British Joint Staff Mission in Washington, DC, and the senior British representative to the Combined Chiefs of Staff. He was aged 62. Dill had served with distinction in his delicate role, a consensus builder skilled in the art of compromise and highly respected among his American peers, including US Army Chief of Staff General George C. Marshall, who is also a close advisor to President Franklin D. Roosevelt.

Dill, formerly Chief of the Imperial General Staff (CIGS), and Prime Minister Winston Churchill had failed to forge a solid working relationship, and just as it appeared that Dill's military career was over in late 1941, when he was removed from the CIGS post and appointed governor-designate of Bombay in far-off India, a fortuitous recollection occurred.

Field Marshal Sir Alan Brooke, Dill's protégé and successor as CIGS, remembered how well the officer had gotten along with the Americans that August during the historic conference at Placentia Bay, Newfoundland, which produced the Atlantic Charter. Brooke paid a visit to Churchill and suggested that Dill accompany the Prime Minister on his December 1941 visit to Washington to confer with Roosevelt in the wake of the Pearl Harbor attack that brought the US into World War Two.

Subsequently, Dill demonstrated superb diplomatic skill and acumen while essentially serving as Britain's military ambassador to the United States. He cultivated a level of mutual trust with the Americans that might well be characterised as transcending even that of Churchill and Roosevelt in that its day-to-day effectiveness was consistently crucial to the ongoing war effort. Dill and Marshall, therefore, overcame differences that might have otherwise strained the Anglo-American relationship to breaking point.

For example, Dill effectively brokered the compromise at the Casablanca Conference that led to the invasion of Sicily rather than a cross-Channel assault on Nazi-occupied Europe in 1943. Brooke noted, "I owe him an unbounded debt of gratitude for his help on that occasion and in many other similar ones." Dill was present during high-level discussions at Casablanca, Quebec, Cairo, and Tehran, and other meetings in Brazil, India, and China just during 1943.

When Dill died, the Americans were shaken. President Roosevelt called the British officer "…the most important figure in the

This equestrian statue at Arlington National Cemetery honours Field Marshal Sir John Dill. (US Government via Wikimedia Commons)

remarkable accord which has been developed in the combined operations of our two countries."

A grief-stricken Marshall made arrangements for the unprecedented burial of a foreign soldier in Arlington National Cemetery, the shrine to America's war heroes. He wrote to Dill's widow: "I know that it is not necessary for me to tell you of my distress of mind at this moment. Officially the United States has suffered a heavy loss, and I personally have lost a dear friend, unique in my lifetime, and never to be out of my mind."

The field marshal was awarded the US Distinguished Service Medal and acclaimed with a joint resolution of the Congress. In 1950, he was further honoured with a magnificent equestrian statue at Arlington, one of only two in the entire cemetery.

Left: Field Marshal Sir John Dill stands third from left at the Placentia Bay Conference, August 1941. General George C. Marshall is to his right. (US Navy via Wikimedia Commons)

Right: Field Marshal Sir John Dill played a key role in Anglo-American relations during World War Two. (Collections of the Imperial War Museums via Wikimedia Commons)

FRANKLIN D. ROOSEVELT ELECTED TO FOURTH TERM

Although the results were somewhat closer than previous presidential elections since 1932, Franklin D. Roosevelt was elected to an unprecedented fourth term as President of the United States. FDR prevailed over Republican nominee Thomas E. Dewey, governor of New York. Roosevelt carries 36 states, receives just over 53% of the popular vote, and easily won in the electoral college tabulation, 432-99.

Unlike 1940, Roosevelt did not hesitate to declare for re-election in 1944. Determined to stay the course through to victory in World War Two, he believed that continuity would best serve the interests of the American people. During the Democratic convention, Vice President Henry A. Wallace was replaced on the ticket by Missouri Senator Harry S. Truman. The political move was largely due to Wallace's progressive policies, which the Democratic leadership feared might alienate more conservative members of the party, particularly in the southern states.

While most of Dewey's support had come from the states of the upper Midwest, the outcome of the election was no doubt influenced by the visible decline in FDR's health and his frail appearance. However, Roosevelt had become a national father figure, guiding the nation through the economic woes of the Great

This patriotic 1944 campaign poster promoted a fourth term for Franklin D. Roosevelt as President of the United States. (National Archives and Records Administration via Wikimedia Commons)

Depression and thus far through the turmoil and angst of global war. Regardless of ongoing health challenges, Roosevelt campaigned vigorously. His optimism and good nature were ever present, as was his classic grin that gave heart to the people.

Inauguration day, January 20, 1945, was raw in Washington, DC. Sleet and snow pelted down, and FDR's speech was the shortest since the days of George Washington, just 556 words and six minutes in length. He told the gathering, "In the days and in the years that are to come we shall work for a just and honourable peace, a durable peace, as today we work and fight for total victory. We can and we will achieve such a peace…And so today, in this year of war, 1945, we have learned lessons – at fearful cost – and we shall profit by them…We have learned that we cannot live alone, at peace; that our own well-being is dependent on the well-being of other nations far away. We have learned that we must live as men, not as ostriches, nor as dogs in the manger. We have learned to be citizens of the world, members of the human community."

As President Roosevelt spoke, Allied forces were pressing toward victory on all fronts. However, he would not live to see the day of ultimate triumph, dying of a cerebral haemorrhage on April 12, 1945, just weeks into his fourth term.

Left: Republican nominee Thomas Dewey, governor of New York, lost to Franklin D. Roosevelt in the presidential election of 1944. (Philippe Halsman Library of Congress via Wikimedia Commons)

Below: In October 1944, President Franklin D. Roosevelt waves his hat to the crowd at Soldier Field in Chicago while on the campaign trail for a fourth term. (Franklin Delano Roosevelt Presidential Library via Wikimedia Commons)

BATTLESHIP *TIRPITZ* SUNK

On November 12, 1944 the 42,900-ton Nazi battleship *Tirpitz* was sunk at anchor near the city of Tromso, Norway, by heavy bombers of the Royal Air Force.

Thirty Avro Lancaster bombers of No. 9 Squadron and No. 617 Squadron RAF dropped massive 12,000lb 'Tallboy' bombs on the battleship, long considered a critical threat to Allied convoy traffic during the Battle of the Atlantic. The first bombs missed their target, but seconds later a large explosion was observed on the foredeck of *Tirpitz*, and at least two Tallboys had found their mark. A column of smoke rose 300ft into the air, and a tremendous explosion wracked the battleship as ammunition magazines detonated. About 10 minutes after the first bomb struck home, *Tirpitz* capsized, claiming the lives of approximately 1,000 crewmen. All the RAF bombers returned safely to their bases in England.

Tirpitz, the sister of the famed battleship *Bismarck*, had been a priority for the British Admiralty and the RAF since it became operational in early 1941. An impressive array of armament included eight 15in guns, a dozen 5.9in guns, and an assortment of smaller calibre weapons capable of anti-aircraft defence, as well as eight torpedo tubes. Protected by armour up to 14in thick, the battleship was sleek and fast, with a top speed of 30kts. Its complement included more than 2,000 officers and ratings.

Repeated attempts to bomb the battleship had been less than successful with only some damage inflicted from time to time, although attempts to sortie and engage Allied convoys were frustrated by fuel shortages, British aircraft, and other factors. However, the mere presence of *Tirpitz*, poised to threaten Allied shipping, compelled the British to continue efforts to sink her.

One of the most courageous missions of World War Two was intended to cripple or sink *Tirpitz* while the battleship was anchored in Norway's Kaafjord. For some time, the Royal Navy had been

The massive hull of *Tirpitz* is shown during launching ceremonies at the port of Wilhelmshaven. (Bundesarchiv Bild via Wikimedia Commons)

Escorted by destroyers, the battleship *Tirpitz* is shown underway in Norwegian waters in 1942. (Bundesarchiv Bild via Wikimedia Commons)

experimenting with midget submarines, dubbed X-craft. These small submersibles were 51ft long, weighed 34 tons, and accommodated a crew of four in cramped quarters.

Code named Operation Source, the mission to sink or disable *Tirpitz* was executed in September 1943. The X-craft were intended to penetrate the anti-submarine defences at Kaafjord and detach their 'side cargoes', pairs of two-ton explosive Amitol charges. These would be timed to detonate after the attackers had cleared the vicinity.

Although X-craft were lost during the perilous voyage across the North Sea and to German fire during the raid, explosive charges were jettisoned, and explosions rocked *Tirpitz*, tearing a gaping hole in the battleship's hull, wrecking steering gear, and dislodging the 15in guns from their mounts. *Tirpitz* was put out of action for more than six months.

Ten X-craft crewmen were killed during Operation Source, while Lieutenant Duncan Cameron and Lieutenant Godfrey Place received the Victoria Cross.

During one of numerous British raids, *Tirpitz* is shown under attack by planes of the Royal Navy Fleet Air Arm in the spring of 1944. (Collections of the Imperial War Museums via Wikimedia Commons)

BRITISH PACIFIC FLEET ESTABLISHED

After retiring to the western reaches of the Indian Ocean in 1942, two years later the British Royal Navy was organised to return to the Pacific theatre. Some controversy surrounds the Royal Navy participation in the Pacific War, which had up to now been almost exclusively an American naval endeavour.

When the British government extended an offer to send major assets to the Pacific in the spring of 1944, President Franklin D. Roosevelt accepted enthusiastically, although the reception from his chief of naval operations, Admiral Ernest J. King and other high-ranking officers of the US Navy was subdued at best. British leaders recognised the dynamic posed and understood that the Royal Navy presence would require a standalone operational capability, including resupply and

Royal Navy Admiral Sir Bruce Fraser, one of the most capable Allied naval officers of World War Two, led the British Pacific Fleet. (Royal Navy via Wikimedia Commons)

logistics. British naval officers further faced the condition that their contribution would be subordinate to the US role. In fact, the US Navy had eclipsed the Royal Navy in terms of sheer size during the war years as well.

The British Pacific Fleet was constituted with early headquarters at Ceylon and then relocated to Sydney, Australia, with a forward base at Manus in the Admiralty Islands. Admiral Bruce Fraser, hero of the Battle of the North Cape, was elevated from command of the Eastern Fleet to that of the Pacific Fleet, and in time the Royal Navy presence in theatre rose to six fleet aircraft carriers, five battleships, 15 light, escort, and maintenance carriers, 11 cruisers, 35 destroyers, dozens of other ships, and more than 750 aircraft.

The British Pacific Fleet operated against the Japanese in the East Indies, during the invasion of Okinawa, and elsewhere, capably led by Adm Fraser, who flew his flag aboard the battleship *Howe*. Fraser was perhaps the most popular of British officers among the American allies. His affable personality, understanding of the US 'senior' role in the Pacific, and experience were key elements in the cooperation exhibited during the waning months of the war with Japan.

Fraser assessed the situation and later concluded, "It was clear that in the intensive, efficient and hard striking type of war that the US fleet was fighting nothing but the inclusion of a big British force would be noticeable and nothing but the best would be tolerated." Fraser got along well with his US co-belligerents and often found himself entertaining American guests aboard his flagship. Alcohol was prohibited aboard ships of the US Navy, but there were opportunities to come calling at appropriate times.

While the Royal Navy proved its worth in action, enduring Japanese kamikaze suicide attacks and conducting extensive air sorties and shore bombardment tasks, Fraser excelled not only as a naval officer, but also as a de facto diplomat.

Admiral Chester Nimitz, the US Commander-in-Chief Pacific Ocean Areas, warmed to Fraser, and the two considered themselves personal friends. Nimitz once remarked that he visited with Fraser "… partly on official business, partly because I like him, and mostly to get a Scotch and soda before dinner…."

Royal Navy aircraft carriers *Indomitable*, *Indefatigable*, *Unicorn*, *Illustrious*, *Victorious*, and *Formidable* are seen at anchor in the Pacific. (Royal Navy via Wikimedia Commons)

Smoke billows from HMS *Formidable* after the carrier was struck by a Japanese kamikaze off Okinawa in May 1945. (Royal Navy via Wikimedia Commons)

FIRST B-29 RAID ON JAPAN FROM MARIANAS

Above: A B-29 Superfortress of the 39th Bombardment Group drops incendiaries on a target in Japan during a daylight raid. (United States Army Air Force via Wikimedia Commons)

Right: From the Marianas, General Curtis LeMay led the US bombing campaign against the Japanese home islands. (US Air Force via Wikimedia Commons)

Once US Marines and US Army troops had captured the islands of Saipan, Guam, and Tinian in the Marianas archipelago, the Allies had a base roughly 1,500 miles from the home islands of Japan. It meant that the first major air raid on Japan itself could be conducted by US Army Air Forces Boeing B-29 Superfortress heavy bombers. On this day in 1944 the force struck the Nakajima Aircraft Engine Plant at Musashino, in suburban Tokyo. B-29s of the 73rd Wing, XXI Bomber Command, XX Air Force begin a concerted air campaign to devastate Japanese industrial capacity and destroy the enemy's major cities.

The seizure of the Marianas in June-July 1944 brought the home islands within range of the B-29s, and construction of airfields on Guam, Tinian, and Saipan was underway rapidly. The B-29s were deployed from their training bases in the United States to the Marianas under the command of General Haywood Hansell. In 1945, Hansell was succeeded by General Curtis LeMay, previously commander of XX Bomber Command in the China-Burma-India Theatre. As LeMay took control of XXI Bomber Command and XX Air Force, he was responsible for vigorously prosecuting the bombing campaign against Japan.

After rather disappointing results during high-altitude bombing raids due to ongoing cloud cover, drift caused by the high winds of the jet stream, and Japanese air defences, LeMay reevaluated the US bombing tactics. LeMay switched from high-altitude daylight bombing to low-altitude night attacks. The big B-29s were stripped of unnecessary weight, including defensive machine guns, and packed full of incendiary bombs intended to start raging fires in Japanese cities whose structures were built mainly of wood.

Following the tactical shift, bombing raids were conducted against 67 Japanese cities, wreaking incredible destruction. The most notable of these B-29 raids was against Tokyo, the Japanese capital, on the night of March 9-10, 1945. For three hours, waves of 325 B-29s dropped 1,665 tons of incendiaries on the city, killing an estimated 100,000 people and laying waste to 16 sq miles of Tokyo.

During the final months of World War Two in the Pacific, the Marianas airfields served as the staging area for LeMay's bombing campaign that is believed to have eventually destroyed roughly 40% of the inhabited areas of dozens of Japanese cities, inflicted half a million casualties, and seriously crippled the enemy's industrial capacity. Although the raids were controversial, LeMay defended the tactic, commenting, "…if the war is shortened by a single day, the attack will have served its purpose…."

B-29s flying from Tinian also delivered the atomic bombs on Hiroshima and Nagasaki in August 1945, that brought the final surrender of Japan and the end of World War Two.

Boeing B-29 Superfortress bombers of the US 29th Bombardment Group are shown at North Field on the island of Guam in 1945. (United States Air Force via Wikimedia Commons)

The Japanese aircraft carrier *Shinano* is shown underway during sea trials in Tokyo Bay, November 1944. (Government of Japan via Wikimedia Commons)

USS ARCHERFISH SINKS SHINANO

Sixty-five miles off the coast of the home island of Honshu, the mammoth Japanese aircraft carrier *Shinano* was struck by four Mark 14 torpedoes fired from the Balao-class submarine USS *Archerfish*. Although Captain Toshio Abe believed at first that the 72,000-ton carrier would survive, a pronounced 20° list to starboard persisted, and as the *Shinano*'s pumps failed it became apparent that the carrier was doomed.

Shinano had been en route from the Yokosuka naval shipyard on the western shore of Tokyo Bay to the port city of Kure on the Inland Sea to take on its complement of fighter and bomber aircraft in addition to a number of Ohka suicide planes and Shinyo speed boats that were already aboard. It was the big carrier's maiden voyage, and the last hopes of the Japanese naval high command were with her upcoming deployment. The Japanese believed that the sudden appearance of a 'super carrier' might shake the Americans in the Philippines and the central Pacific, disrupting operations and perhaps buying the Empire precious time.

Shinano had originally been intended as the third 'super battleship' of the Imperial Japanese Navy, a sister to *Musashi*, sunk at the Battle of Leyte Gulf, and *Yamato*, which had sustained damage there and was later sent to the bottom of the Pacific during a one-way mission in the battle for the island of Okinawa. However, after the disastrous loss of four aircraft carriers at the Battle of Midway in 1942, the decision was made to convert the third battleship hull to an aircraft carrier, and orders were given to complete construction with all haste. An accident during construction in October 1944, led to a delay and gave rise to the feeling that the big carrier was jinxed.

On the night of November 28, 1944, *Shinano* was at sea. Numerous reports indicated that American submarines were active off the home islands, and

The submarine USS *Archerfish* sank the Japanese aircraft carrier *Shinano* with four torpedoes off the coast of Honshu. (US Navy via Wikimedia Commons)

Captain Abe was wary of attack, although he ordered three escorting destroyers to remain close by rather than chasing down any visual or sonar contacts.

Meanwhile, *Archerfish*, under Commander Joseph Enright, had set out from Pearl Harbor on October 5, on the submarine's fifth war patrol. *Archerfish* made contact with an unidentified surface ship on the evening of November 28. Enright initially thought that he was shadowing a large tanker, but later visual assessment by periscope revealed that the target was indeed an aircraft carrier.

Enright manoeuvred into position in the predawn hours of November 29 and ordered the firing of a spread of four torpedoes. The first ripped into the carrier's stern, while three more found their target at eight-second intervals. Four gaping holes were slashed into *Shinano*. The starboard engine room, firerooms, air compressor room, and other compartments were rapidly flooded.

After struggling for seven hours to keep the carrier afloat, Abe ordered the crew off the sinking *Shinano*. He went down with the ship, one of 1,435 men who died. *Shinano* remains the largest warship ever sunk in combat by a submarine.

Enright and the crew of *Archerfish* made good their escape.

Commander Joseph Enright served as skipper of USS *Archerfish* during the stalk and sinking of *Shinano*. (US Navy via Wikimedia Commons)

PALAWAN MASSACRE

A sign warns that the area where the Japanese have buried Palawan Massacre victims is off limits. (Bob Meza via Wikimedia Commons)

Stories of Japanese atrocities during World War Two are common, but one of the worst took place on December 14 on the island of Palawan in the western Philippines. As many as 150 American prisoners were herded into air raid shelters, doused with gasoline, and burned to death. The atrocity took place near the town of Puerta Princesa and was sanctioned by Japanese officers. Those prisoners who manage to briefly escape from the deathtraps were hunted down, shot, or bayoneted and left to die.

The POWs, some of whom were captured during the fighting at the Bataan Peninsula and the island of Corregidor in the spring of 1942, had been used as forced labour to build and maintain a 3,000-yard-long airstrip, performing such tasks as clearing large trees, pouring concrete, and repairing bomb damage sustained during American air raids. Living conditions were deplorable. Rations were scarcely enough to sustain life; disease was rampant; water was scarce. Those who were physically unable to work or sought any relief from their brutal captors were typically murdered on the spot.

A group of 346 American POWs had been brought to Palawan from a prison in Manila in August 1942, and in September 1944, the Japanese ordered more than half those left alive to return to the capital city as work on the airstrip neared completion. In October, US troops began the liberation of the Philippines, landing on the central island of Leyte under the command of General Douglas MacArthur. The Japanese commander at Palawan sought instructions on the disposition of the POWs in his charge should the Americans approach.

The response from higher-echelon officers was chilling. "Whether they are destroyed individually or in groups…dispose of them as the situation dictates," the order read. On the terrible day of the massacre, the Americans were brought to the airstrip as usual. Sometime later, Japanese guards abruptly ordered them to stop working and to pack themselves tightly into three shelters roughly five feet deep and four feet wide and another that was much smaller.

Five soldiers emptied cans of aviation fuel into the first shelter, and two others ignited the flames with torches. Those who tried to escape were immediately cut down. Amid the screams and rifle reports, some others in the remaining trenches attempted to flee but met similar fates. That evening, Filipinos reportedly witnessed a Japanese celebration of the grisly affair and noted that they bragged of killing 149 of the 150 Americans present.

General MacArthur received a report of the massacre in January 1945 and issued a stern warning to Japanese officers that they would be held accountable for their reprehensible conduct. After the war, 33 Japanese soldiers were charged with war crimes related to the Palawan Massacre. Sixteen were convicted and sentenced to prison. One death sentence was commuted to 30 years behind bars. All were released by 1958.

A cross marks the grave where victims of the Palawan Massacre are being interred. (US Army Signal Corps via Wikimedia Commons)

The entrance to the Plaza Cuartel at Puerta Princesa on the Philippine island of Palawan, site of the 1944 massacre, is pictured decades after the infamous atrocity. (Pi3. 124 via Wikimedia Commons)

GLENN MILLER GOES MISSING

On December 15, US Army Air Forces Major Glenn Miller, famed the world over as a swing musician and big band leader, disappeared. Miller was on a flight from Twinwood Farm, an RAF airstrip near Bedford, bound for Paris. With him were another passenger, Colonel Norman F. Baesell, and pilot Flight Officer F.O. Morgan.

Miller had intended to make advance arrangements for the forthcoming arrival of his Army Air Forces band in France and to prepare for a Christmas Eve concert that would be aired on the BBC. On a rainy Friday afternoon, he arrived at the airstrip and boarded the single-engine, eight passenger Noorduyn Norseman C-64 monoplane. Miller disliked flying and was particularly nervous about the small plane.

Reportedly, Miller joked: "Where the hell are the parachutes?" Baesell retorted, "What's the matter, Miller? Do you want to live forever?" Miller also had made an earlier ominous comment to George Voutsas, director of the bandleader's military radio programming. "I don't know why I spend time making plans like this," Miller remarked. "You know, George, I have an awful feeling you guys are going to go home without me."

Despite the inclement weather and posted warnings, the small aircraft rumbled down the runway and into the air – never to be seen again. Exactly what happened to the Norseman and its three occupants remains one of the enduring mysteries of the 20th century.

Glenn Miller plays the trombone while leading his famous band circa 1940.
(US Government via Wikimedia Commons)

Allied officials assumed that the small plane had experienced engine trouble or that ice buildup on the airframe had caused it to crash into the English Channel. There was little official news of the plane's disappearance until just after 6pm on Christmas Eve when the BBC noted, "Major Glenn Miller, the well-known American bandleader, is reported missing. He left England for Paris nine days ago."

Miller was subsequently declared dead, and in February 1945, he was posthumously awarded the Bronze Star.

Numerous theories and wild speculation as to the fate of Glenn Miller have persisted through the years, and after his death his music remained popular. Hits like *Chattanooga Choo Choo*, *In the Mood*, *String of Pearls*, *Moonlight Serenade*, and many others remain iconic examples of swing music and the Big Band Era. In four years, Miller's civilian band charted 16 number one hit songs and 69 that reached the top 10. At the time he joined the armed forces, Miller was at the zenith of his career. At age 38 and requiring prescription eyeglasses, it was not likely that he would be called up to serve. The army accepted his offer to engage in "a real job in the army" and his interest in "streamlining modern military music."

The name of Major Alton Glenn Miller is listed in the Tablets of the Missing at Cambridge American Cemetery and Memorial in Cambridge, England, and a memorial stone is located in Arlington National Cemetery.

Famed band leader Glenn Miller went missing during a flight from England to Paris in 1944.
(Billboard Magazine Unknown Author via Wikimedia Commons)

A Noorduyn Norseman aircraft similar to this example was lost with Glenn Miller aboard. (US Air Force via Wikimedia Commons)

BATTLE OF THE BULGE BEGINS

A t 5:30am on December 16, 1944, hundreds of German guns opened a blistering artillery barrage, and the target is the American line in the dense Ardennes Forest, an unlikely place for a German offensive due to the difficult terrain and heavily wooded landscape. However, Adolf Hitler had unleashed Operation Watch on the Rhine, a desperate gamble to turn the tide of military adversity recently experience by the German armed forces on the Western Front.

Against the advice of his cadre of field marshals and generals, for months Hitler had plotted the winter offensive that developed into the famous Battle of the Bulge. At last, by mid-December 1944 he had assembled 275,000 troops, nearly 700 tanks, and 2,000 artillery pieces. The aim of the thrust was to split the Allied 12th and 21st Army Groups, under General Omar Bradley and Field Marshal Bernard Montgomery respectively, driving a wedge between them, then racing for key crossings of the River Meuse and on to the great port of Antwerp, Belgium, second largest in Europe and a nexus of Allied resupply during the drive into the Third Reich.

Hitler reasoned that if Antwerp could be taken, the blow might be so severe as to create disruption among the Allied leaders and result even in an opportunity for a favourable peace settlement with the West. If that were accomplished the Nazi military could then turn again swiftly to deal with the Soviet Red Army, massing on the Eastern Front for an expected offensive across the River Vistula and into the heart of the Fatherland.

While the German military leadership deemed the Führer's plan delusional, Hitler focussed on marshalling forces to execute the Ardennes offensive, even transferring infantry and panzer divisions from the Soviet front to bolster the sledgehammer blow that was to fall against a quiet and thinly-manned sector of the Allied line stretching through

A soldier of the Nazi SS shows the strain of combat during the Battle of the Bulge. (US Government via Wikimedia Commons)

German soldiers dash across a road while abandoned American equipment lies in the background. (National Archives and Records Administration via Wikimedia Commons)

the forest from the town of Echternach, Luxembourg, in the south to Monschau, Germany, in the north – a front of 60 miles.

Hitler unleashed three armies, north to south, Sixth Panzer under SS General Joseph 'Sepp' Dietrich, Fifth Panzer under General Hasso von Manteuffel, and the Seventh under General Erich Brandenberger. The Nazi thrust was a total surprise to the Allies, although ominous signs of an enemy buildup of strength near the Ardennes had been noted and then shrugged off. German spearheads made good progress, but pockets of American resistance slowed the dash for the Meuse, particularly where the US 99th Infantry Division was dug in along Elsenborn Ridge.

Dietrich ordered a shift to the south and outflanked some American positions on the Schnee Eifel, a cluster of wooded hillocks and small villages. While some US soldiers clung stubbornly to Elsenborn Ridge, others surrendered in droves at the Schnee Eifel. The previously untested 106th Infantry

An American soldier surveys the scene of the Malmedy Massacre after the Battle of the Bulge. (US National Oceanic and Atmospheric Administration via Wikimedia Commons)

An American M36 tank destroyer rolls forward to fight the German advance during the Battle of the Bulge. (US Army via Wikimedia Commons)

Division was cut off, and on December 19, two full regiments were marched into captivity.

Meanwhile, SS Lieutenant Colonel Joachim Peiper led the vanguard of Dietrich's panzers toward the Meuse but ran into small groups of US Army engineers who frustrated his progress. Peiper was enraged when his lead tank was knocked out and his armoured column stalled for hours near the bridge across the River Ambleve at Stavelot, Belgium. Peiper's men gained lasting infamy with the massacre of 85 American prisoners from the 285th Field Artillery Observation Battalion in a desolate field near the Belgian town of Malmedy.

Not only was Peiper vexed by small groups of gallant engineers, but his motorised mission was plagued by fuel shortages. When Kampfgruppe (Battle Group) Peiper was finally halted, Allied counterblows decimated the Germans; only 800 of his original complement of 4,000 troops managed to avoid being killed, wounded, or captured. Building on their holdouts at Elsenborn Ridge, the Allies reinforced positions and established a strong northern shoulder against the 'bulge'. Montgomery was given temporary command of forces to the north to facilitate troop movements.

In the south, Brandenberger ran into veteran Americans of the 9th Armored and 4th Infantry Divisions and made no appreciable headway. However, in the centre Manteuffel's tanks came the closest to their objective only to be slowed for six days by elements of the US 7th Armored Division that made a heroic stand at the town of St. Vith, Belgium. The stalwarts at St. Vith were forced to surrender

on December 23, but they bought Montgomery precious time to consolidate his defences. Meanwhile, the German offensive reached its high-water mark at Foy-Notre-Dame, southeast of Dinant, Belgium, and the Meuse bridges there.

Further to the southwest, the US 101st Airborne Division, elements of Combat Command B, 10th Armored Division, and other forces held the crossroads town of Bastogne, Belgium, for several critical days against the Germans. General Anthony McAuliffe, acting commander of the 101st, refused a surrender ultimatum. At the same time, General George S. Patton, Jr., promised to come to the relief of Bastogne and then delivered in spades.

Patton's Third Army was engaged in a fight through the Saar, but with orders from General Dwight Eisenhower, supreme commander of Allied forces, Patton disengaged on December 20, pivoted his vanguard 90o, and struck north toward Bastogne. The 4th Armored Division and the beleaguered paratroopers made contact on the day after Christmas.

By late December, Hitler's bold stroke had shot its bolt. Clearing weather allowed Allied aircraft to strafe and bomb German formations. Ground troops battered the enemy salient, compelling the Germans to retreat. By January 15, 1945, the 'bulge' had been reduced, and with it Hitler's grandiose dream of victory in the West.

The Nazis shattered their sword during the Battle of the Bulge, losing 120,000 casualties and scores of irreplaceable armoured vehicles – then unavailable to face the coming Red Army onslaught in the East. American casualties were heavy, with 8,500 dead, 46,000 wounded, and 20,000 taken prisoner. Unlike the Germans, however, the Americans could make good their losses. The Allied victory in the Battle of the Bulge, therefore, hastened the defeat of the Third Reich.

American combat engineers, after holding their position against German attacks during the Battle of the Bulge, head for a rest. (National Archives and Records Administration via Wikimedia Commons)

A German soldier is escorted into captivity after his PzKpfw. V Panther medium tank was knocked out during fighting on Elsenborn Ridge. (US Army Signal Corps via Wikimedia Commons)

TYPHOON BATTERS HALSEY'S THIRD FLEET

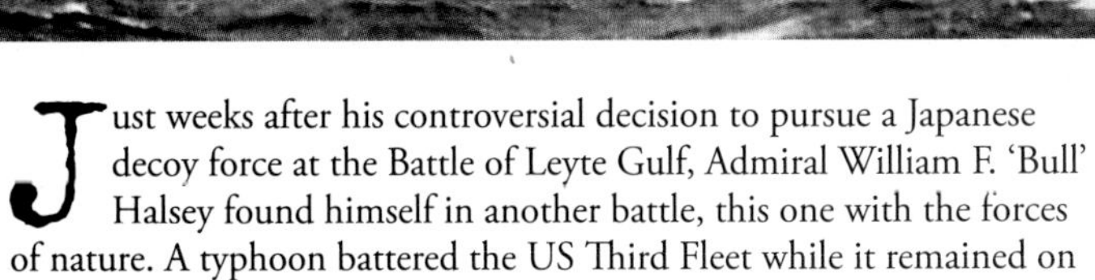

The light carrier USS *Langley* rocks during the typhoon of December 18, 1944. (US Navy National Museum of Naval Aviation via Wikimedia Commons)

The bow of the battleship USS *Massachusetts* ploughs through heavy seas off the Philippines during the December 1944 typhoon. (US Navy via Wikimedia Commons)

Just weeks after his controversial decision to pursue a Japanese decoy force at the Battle of Leyte Gulf, Admiral William F. 'Bull' Halsey found himself in another battle, this one with the forces of nature. A typhoon battered the US Third Fleet while it remained on station in Philippine waters.

Halsey had received some conflicting reports of the typhoon's course but chose to continue refuelling operations as time slipped away with the storm's approach. A day earlier, he had observed the destroyer USS *Spence* rolling amid rough seas while refuelling from the battleship USS *New Jersey*, his flagship. The disturbance was so intense that it appeared the destroyer might actually collide with the battleship. "She was riding up ahead," the admiral recalled of the little destroyer, "and she'd drop well astern and charge ahead and drop astern…She was pitching and rolling heavily."

Nearly two hours later, Halsey ordered a halt to the refuelling operations. Contemplating the best course of action, including the necessity to provide support for General Douglas MacArthur's ground troops in the Philippines, Halsey ordered a course change from due west to due south on the night of December 17. Although he sought calmer waters to resume the critical refuelling effort, Halsey

had unknowingly ordered his task force directly into the teeth of the typhoon, its strength steadily growing.

Barometric pressure fell rapidly, and winds rose to 73kts as 70ft waves pounded the Third Fleet on the morning of December 18. Halsey sent a weather warning to the fleet and later recalled, "We were completely cornered. The consideration then was the fastest way to get out of the dangerous semicircle and to get to a position where our destroyers could be refuelled."

Before the typhoon subsided, three destroyers were sunk, 146 aircraft were lost, and 802 sailors were killed. The light aircraft carrier *Monterey* and escort carrier *Kwajalein* temporarily lost steerage, while the light carrier *Independence* had two seamen swept overboard. The small destroyers and destroyer escorts were the most vulnerable of Halsey's ships. The destroyers *Hull*, *Spence*, and *Monaghan* capsized and carried virtually all hands to bottom of the roiling sea.

A court of inquiry was later convened and concluded that Halsey had made an error in judgement. However, he received no formal reprimand or sanction. Remarkably, a second typhoon struck the Third Fleet in January 1945, and a second court of inquiry recommended that Halsey be reassigned. However, the political fallout of such an action apparently outweighed the gravity of the incident. Halsey was one of the great heroes of the Pacific War, and a black mark on the reputation of such a prominent figure might adversely affect morale. Again, no punitive action was taken.

Admiral William F. 'Bull' Halsey, who led the Third Fleet into a heavy typhoon, talks with Admiral Chester Nimitz, Commander-in-Chief Pacific Ocean Areas. (US Navy via Wikimedia Commons)

SS *LEOPOLDVILLE* SUNK

At the height of the Battle of the Bulge, the troopship SS *Leopoldville* was torpedoed and sunk by the German submarine *U-486*. Aboard the stricken vessel, lying just five miles off the French port of Cherbourg after embarking from Southampton, were more than 2,000 American soldiers of the 262nd and 264th Regiments, 66th Infantry Division. These troops were meant as reinforcements to fight the Germans during the great but desperate enemy offensive; instead, many of them were fighting for their lives in the frigid waters of the Atlantic.

Some of the Americans were killed outright by the pair of torpedo blasts that doomed the *Leopoldville*, while others succumbed to hypothermia before they could be pulled from the water. In the end, 756 US soldiers and 56 members of the *Leopoldville* crew lost their lives on that terrible Christmas Eve. Compounding the difficulties encountered were a shortage of lifejackets and the language barrier that hardly anyone had been concerned about. The order to abandon the Belgian ship had been given in Flemish. Amid the confusion, some soldiers did find their way to lifeboats, but others remained aboard the *Leopoldville* believing that the ship was only slightly damaged and would soon be towed into port.

The escorting destroyer HMS *Brilliant* was first to come alongside the stricken troopship and render aid. Its crew brought approximately 500 men to safety. However, amid the confusion no other ships approached the area until it was too late to save many more. Some personnel ashore at Cherbourg scarcely gave notice to the tragedy that was unfolding before them on Christmas Eve. Many were distracted with holiday observances, and more than an hour elapsed before any rescue vessels departed Cherbourg to provide rescue assistance.

American soldier Orland B. Herrington was serving as a cook in Cherbourg and remembered the grim tasks that were undertaken as the magnitude of the tragedy was finally realised. "Our company was called into service to haul the injured to a hospital some distance away and to haul the dead to a morgue," he wrote. "Those who were just in need of warm, dry clothing and food were taken to various units where they could find assistance…."

An extensive news blackout followed the *Leopoldville* disaster as both the British and American governments sought to avoid publicity surrounding the ineptitude and unfortunate circumstances that had occurred. Soldiers of the 66th Division were told not to speak of the incident, and even after discharge they were required to remain silent. Decades later, a History Channel documentary described the sinking of the *Leopoldville* and subsequent cover-up in detail.

This poster advertises prewar pleasure cruises aboard the SS *Leopoldville*. (Compagnie maritime belge du Congo via Wikimedia Commons)

Left: Major General Herman F. Kramer was in command of the 66th Infantry Division when tragedy struck aboard the SS *Leopoldville*. (US Army via Wikimedia Commons)

Below: The German submarine *U-486* was a Type VII-C U-boat similar to the *U-995* on display at the naval museum near Kiel, Germany. (Darkone via Wikimedia Commons)

BASTOGNE RELIEVED

As the lead tanks of the 37th Infantry Battalion rumbled through snow and ice toward the besieged Belgian crossroads town of Bastogne, the defenders in the vicinity hurled themselves into the nearest foxholes ready to fight. In one of the leading M4 Sherman medium tanks, Lieutenant Charles Boggess stood up in his turret and shouted, "Come here! This is the 4th Armored!" An American helmet poked up, and an unshaven, fatigued officer found the courage to approach, his finger firmly on the trigger of his M1 carbine. Convinced, he shouted back, "Second Lieutenant Duane J. Webster, 326th Engineer Battalion, 101st Airborne Division!"

The epic siege of Bastogne was over.

Ten days after the Germans launched the Ardennes Offensive, Hitler's desperate gamble in the west popularly known as the Battle of the Bulge, the key defenders of Bastogne have withstood an almost continual onslaught of German infantry and armour attacks, artillery shelling, and even a raid by Luftwaffe bombers. The courage of the 101st Airborne Division, Combat Command B of the 10th Armored Division, and elements of several other units had paid off, slowing the German advance toward the port of Antwerp and helping to thwart the Führer's grand design to split the Allied 12th and 21st Army Groups.

For the Germans, the seizure of Bastogne would have meant access to a road network that would facilitate their westward advance. Three Wehrmacht divisions, 2nd Panzer, Panzer Lehr, and the 26th Volksgrenadier were ordered to take the town at all costs. General Dwight Eisenhower, commanding Allied forces in Western Europe, responded to the threat with the only readily available reserves, the battle-weary 82nd and 101st Airborne Divisions, both recovering from recent fighting in The Netherlands.

While the 82nd was trucked north to bolster defences around the towns of Werbomont and Houffalize, Military Police directing traffic shunted the trucks carrying the 101st southeast to Bastogne. The lightly armed paratroopers at Bastogne went into the line in the early hours of December 19, 1944, their interim commander, Brigadier General Anthony McAuliffe, charged with organising the defences. McAuliffe, the 101st Airborne Division's artillery officer, had taken temporary command while General Maxwell Taylor was thousands of miles away attending meetings in Washington, DC.

As the 101st streamed into Bastogne, its troopers saw a steady flow of soldiers headed toward the rear, disorganised and downtrodden after being surprised by the German offensive. Many of them were without weapons or equipment. To a man, the Screaming Eagles of the 101st realised they were being tossed into a desperate situation.

Within hours, tanks and troops of Panzer Lehr and the 2nd Panzer Division were hitting forward positions and roadblocks in the vicinity of Bastogne, and the town was soon surrounded by German forces. Casualties were heavy on both sides. Enemy artillery was a constant

General George S. Patton, Jr., presents the Distinguished Service Cross to General Anthony McAuliffe for heroism at Bastogne. (US Army via Wikimedia Commons)

Above: Soldiers of the 101st Airborne Division drag supplies airdropped to the defenders of Bastogne into their positions. (US Army Center of Military History via Wikimedia Commons)

Below: American tanks and troops occupy positions around Bastogne after the relief of the embattled defenders during the Battle of the Bulge. (US Army via Wikimedia Commons)

Soldiers of the 101st Airborne Division watch transport aircraft drop supplies to the defenders of Bastogne. (US Army Signal Corps via Wikimedia Commons)

McAuliffe turned to Lieutenant Colonel Joseph Harper, commander of the 327th Glider Regiment, and said, "Will you see that it's delivered?" Harper grinned broadly and said, "I'll deliver it myself."

At last, on December 23, weather conditions improved and Allied fighter-bombers hit German tank and troop concentrations while transport planes of the 241st Troop Carrier Command made hundreds of sorties during the next 48 hours, air-dropping much-needed supplies to sustain the garrison.

Meanwhile, General George S. Patton, Jr.'s Third Army had disengaged from offensive operations in the Saar and turned north toward Bastogne, intent on keeping its commander's promise of relieving Bastogne's embattled defenders. Virtually without pause, Third Army tanks rolled forward day and night, fighting where necessary but skirting around many pockets of resistance or small towns teeming with Germans.

After four days of winter fighting, the spearhead of Patton's army, the 4th Armored Division, neared

threat, and the wounded piled up at aid stations. After several days of fighting, ammunition and supplies were running low, and even medical personnel were few as a large contingent of the 101st detachment had been captured early in the ordeal.

By the morning of December 22, the Germans had bypassed Bastogne, but their advance was slowed considerably. Still confident that the capture of the town was imminent, the Germans made a surrender overture. Sergeant Oswald Butler of the 327th Glider Regiment spotted four enemy soldiers under a flag of truce. Two of them were blindfolded and marched to the nearest company command post. Their message was translated and sent up the American chain of command.

It read in part: "To the U.S.A. commander of the encircled town of Bastogne: The fortune of war is changing. This time the U.S.A. forces in and near Bastogne have been encircled by strong German armoured units. There is only one possibility to save the encircled troops from total annihilation: that is the honourable surrender of the encircled town."

McAuliffe's terse reply shines brightly in the annals of American military lore. He retorted, "To the German Commander: Nuts! The American Commander." After composing the eloquent response,

Bastogne. Commanding the tip of the spear, Lieutenant Colonel Creighton Abrams sent his 37th Tank Battalion, guns blazing, on a sprint through the town of Assenois, finally linking up with the 101st Airborne at Bastogne on the day after Christmas.

Thanks to the heroic defence of Bastogne and gallant stands in other areas, Hitler's winter offensive was stopped. In the coming days Allied counterattacks recaptured all the ground temporarily ceded to the Germans and inflicted severe losses on the enemy, hastening the end of World War Two in Europe. During its famed contribution to the victory, the 101st Airborne lost 1,641 men killed, wounded, or captured. In their sacrifice, the Screaming Eagles had fought one of the great defensive actions of modern military history.

During a January 1945 memorial service for the fallen at Bastogne, American combat engineers fire a ceremonial salute. (US Army via Wikimedia Commons)

American infantrymen move toward Bastogne, firing at the enemy during combat operations in December 1944. (US Army via Wikimedia Commons)

SURGING RED ARMY; JAPANESE SUNSET; BULGE

The atmosphere was somewhat tense during the meeting at Verdun on December 19, 1944. General Dwight D. Eisenhower, commander of Allied forces in Western Europe, had called his lieutenants together at the scene of months of bloodletting during the Great War a generation earlier. The gathering took place amid the gloom of an old stone French Army barracks, and that gloom contributed to the pervasive unsettled feeling amid the German Ardennes Offensive, the epic Battle of the Bulge.

The Western Allies had just recently ended their airborne/ground offensive into The Netherlands, and Operation Market Garden had failed to achieve a crossing of the great River Rhine into Germany. Casualties had been high, and the delayed opening of the port of Antwerp had frustrated the Allied advance into Germany.

Three weeks after Market Garden ended, on December 16, the Nazis had attacked in the Ardennes. Now Eisenhower wanted to know what could be done immediately to stem the Nazi tide in its drive for the River Meuse and to capture Antwerp. A day earlier, General George S. Patton, Jnr, commanding the US Third Army, had met with his boss, 12th Army Group commander General Omar Bradley, in Luxembourg. When Bradley spread a map before Patton and described the depth of the German penetration and the critical dispositions of troops, the latter struck his usual aggressive tone and offered that he could turn Third Army to the north, with two divisions en route to the southern shoulder of the bulge with another following in 24 hours.

Hours later, in the dimly lit barracks at Verdun, Eisenhower looked around the room. He was greeted with some murmurs of

American paratroopers survey the wreckage of a glider during Operation Market Garden. (US Army via Wikimedia Commons)

indecisiveness – except on the part of Patton. While others had come with only undefined ideas, Patton had already worked out three possible plans to attack the bulge from the south. When he repeated the promise made to Bradley while in the presence of Eisenhower, the commander-in-chief responded, "Don' be fatuous George!" But Patton was not hesitant. He turned to Bradley and snarled, "Brad, the Kraut's stuck his head in a meatgrinder. And this time I've got hold of the handle!"

In December 1944, Patton was at the zenith of his charismatic and controversial career. His performance in the perilous hour of the Battle of the Bulge has been retold many times in the decades since. The fighting charge of Third Army to the relief of Bastogne was a key component in the eventual failure of the German offensive that forever quashed Hitler's ambitions for a separate peace with the Western Allies so that he might turn all his military energy toward the scourge of the Soviet Red Army bearing down on the Third Reich from the East.

While the great bulge was being reduced at staggering cost to the Nazis, the Soviets were poised to deliver sledgehammer blows against their former ally turned nemesis. In the summer of 1944, the Soviets

General George S. Patton, Jnr, delivered on his promise to raise the siege of Bastogne during the Battle of the Bulge. (National Portrait Gallery via Wikimedia Commons)

Minsk, the capital city of Belorussia, lay in ruins after its capture by the Red Army. (Vladimir Nikolayevich Ivanov Russian Federation via Wikimedia Commons)

had unleashed Operation Bagration, a massive offensive into Belorussia and eastern Poland. By the end of July, they had reached the outskirts of Warsaw and advanced 450 miles in five weeks, halting along the River Vistula.

The year of Stalin's Ten Victories, though, was not over. In the late summer, the Red Army attacked the Germans in Bessarabia on two fronts. A sweeping advance through southeastern and central Europe followed. Although the Germans tried mightily to stem the Red tide, they could at times barely resist. Romania and Bulgaria switched sides to join the fight against the Nazis, and Soviet forces rolled up the valley of the River Danube into Yugoslavia. Belgrade fell by late October, and at the end of the year Soviet tanks and troops were fighting for control of the Hungarian capital of Budapest. In the north, the Soviets had compelled Finland to agree to an armistice while the Red Army thrust into the Baltic States and pressed on to the frontier of East Prussia.

In the Pacific, General Douglas MacArthur had fought his way back from embarrassing evacuation to Australia and waded ashore at the Philippine island of Leyte in October, announcing his return to the Filipino people. The fight for the liberation of the Philippines was to continue for months, but the outcome was clear. US ground forces battled through jungle and mountains for the balance of 1944. At sea, the great US naval triumph at the Battle of the Philippine Sea in June was followed up with a taut, nerve-wracking victory at the Battle of Leyte Gulf, and across the vast expanse of the ocean the second US

A Japanese bomb splashes astern of the aircraft carrier USS *Enterprise* during the Battle of the Philippine Sea. (National Archives and Records Administration via Wikimedia Commons)

pincer toward the Japanese home islands had reached the Marianas, liberating Saipan, Guam, and Tinian to set the stage for massive air raids that would devastate Japan's industry and set its cities ablaze.

In the China-Burma-India theatre, General William Slim and the 14th Army had their sights on Meiktila, east of the River Irrawaddy, threatening both Mandalay and Rangoon.

Although the cost had been tremendous, the Allies made substantial headway against the Axis across the globe by the end of 1944. At times their efforts and ambitions had been frustrated, even though the major initiative had never been given up. At the end of the pivotal year that had seen victories in D-Day, Bagration, the Philippine Sea, Leyte, and the Marianas, Allied leaders knew that serious fighting remained. However, the outcome of World War Two was no longer in doubt.

Prime Minister Winston Churchill, President Franklin D. Roosevelt, and Soviet Premier Josef Stalin each looked to the future, beyond the continuing conflict, and toward the shaping of the postwar world.

Left: Filipino volunteers carry provisions along a jungle trail during the battle for island of Leyte. (US Department of Defense via Wikimedia Commons)

Below: American tanks form a line in the snow during the defence of St Vith, Belgium, during the Battle of the Bulge. (US Army Signal Corps via Wikimedia Commons)